Oasis of DELIGHT

NANCY GOUDIE

First Edition 2013

ISBN 978-0-9564512-2-4

Concept design by Ray Goudie and Nancy Goudie
Graphic design by Lewis Royal
Photo by Dave Pratt

Published by New Generation Music,
Caedmon Complex,
Bristol Road,
Thornbury,
Bristol,
BS35 3JA,
UK
www.ngm.org.uk

Printed and bound in Great Britain by
TJ International Ltd, Padstow, Cornwall

Unless otherwise stated delight quotations are by Nancy Goudie.

This book is dedicated to the ultimate creator God, who has placed us in his amazing love filled garden to live, treasure and explore his joy, pleasure and delight.

Acknowledgements

As with every book that has ever been written, there are always a number of people to thank for their invaluable input. So, I send my special thanks to:

Ray Goudie, my amazing husband, I really believe this book would not have been complete without your helpful comments and many encouragements. Thank you for your great suggestions and your clever editing – what would I do without you?

Kat Bradford and *Sharon Cann* who spent much of their precious time proof reading the manuscript – you two are so amazing and such giving people. I love you both!

Lewis Royal - you truly are a very talented man and it is always a joy to work with you. Praise God for your creativity and attention to detail.

All at ngm – I love you all so much. You are the most incredible people in the whole world and I love your hunger and passion for God. It's been wonderful to discover together more and more about the pleasures God has for each of us.

Those special people who have allowed me to tell their remarkable stories. I know that as your stories are read, many will discover for themselves just how much God delights in them.

Contents

Delight - the **ultimate place** to live

PREFACE

When this book was just a thought in my mind and the only words I had written were Oasis of Delight, I discovered a word that means delight – Eden. That discovery got my senses going and my excitement soaring! When the Lord created human beings he placed them in a garden in Eden. In other words, he placed his amazing, unique creation in his delight. They were surrounded by delight, they were covered with delight and no matter where they looked they saw and breathed delight. God loved mankind so much that he positioned them to live in his joy, pleasure and delight. This experience was not just designed for Adam and Eve, we too have been placed in his wonderful all encompassing delight.

ZEPHANIAH 3:17 tells us that God takes great delight in each of us. He rejoices over us with singing and finds much pleasure in each of us! We are not worthless individuals, indeed before we were born, God poured his delight into us! Even before we took our first breath, he was drenching us with his love and pleasure. We were created to live, breathe and be covered daily with his delight. The Bible tells us that no matter who we are, each of us is a person of great worth and immense value. There is an invitation within this book for you to explore and come to know more of the depths of his amazing oasis of delight.

There are times in our lives when we need an oasis, a place where we can go to receive a thirst quenching drink for our souls, but it is an altogether different experience to not just visit such a place, but to live in this incredible life-giving oasis. This book is an exploration of what it means to live in the oasis of delight, tasting its fruit, relaxing and relishing in the lush surroundings, being encouraged and built up in the beauty of delight. It will inspire you to enjoy the delightful fruit of intimacy with God and with each other, whilst all the time pointing us towards the day when we will be in the ultimate garden of delight for eternity. If we are able to grasp some of the many seeds planted in this book, then I know we will experience the reality of being drenched with the blessings of delight.

I speak in this book about a time when I heard the Lord sing with delight over me. It was an incredible and awesome experience that I will never forget. It was a sound like no other and when his chords of love vibrated to the depths of my being, I was completely undone with his grace and his pleasure in me. The truth is that the Lord sings over each of us every day. Whether we hear his voice or not, he fills the universe and beyond with his many melodies of love, joy and pleasure in us.

One day, as I was out for a walk with the Lord, I asked him to speak to me. I looked across a field and saw some trees in the distance. As I looked, I concentrated on the weeds that were growing around the bottom of the trees. I said to the Lord, *"What a shame that those trees have such a lot of weeds around them."* The Lord replied, *"Nancy look up and see the immense beauty and majesty that is in each of those trees. They are all so incredibly beautiful. Don't look down; instead look up!"* I looked up and was suddenly blown away by the intense beauty I saw. I could have missed it by concentrating on the problem areas.

So many of us don't see the immense beauty, delight and pleasure there is in God. We don't understand or realise that he is a happy God! We forget that it was he who created pleasure. We don't remember that he is able to deal with everything that bothers us. We don't look up! We concentrate on the 'weeds', giving attention to our needs, difficulties and problems, instead of seeing that our God is the God of the impossible. Let's not concentrate on our 'weeds' but let's look up and concentrate on him.

When we do, our whole perspective changes. Let's delight in him and soak in the sunshine of who he is. Let's embrace the happiness he is and experience the deep pleasure that comes from knowing him. Let's not just glance at him, but really soak in his beauty and know what it truly is like to greatly delight in him. My prayer is that through this book you will not only see him for who he is and know how much he loves and delights in each of us, but you will also hear his voice calling you to live in his oasis of delight.

You will notice as you read through the book that I have based the teaching loosely on GENESIS 1–3. The story contained within these three chapters will cause your senses to erupt with pleasure and your heart to explode with contagious joy, as you allow yourself to experience the God of delight. May your heart burn within you as you let him feed you with his exotic passion and joy whilst you enjoy Eden – his garden of bliss. At the end of each chapter, I have created a place where you can enjoy swimming in and drinking from the river of delights. By completing each suggested spiritual exercise, you will then be in a place where you can enjoy the life giving water, which will spring up within you. I believe God is the source of unending joy and pleasure and therefore as you enjoy him, there is no doubt that you will adore your oasis of delight experience every day!

DELIGHT

GOD – THE ULTIMATE ARTIST!

God is the most amazing artist EVER! You only have to look at the world he created to discover what an incredible artist he is! His colours, his creativity, his shapes, his sounds, his designs, amaze us as we see the incredible depth of beauty in everything he made. Not only did he fashion and create the world in which we live, but also what he did in the rest of the universe is breath-taking! Planets and galaxies were made by his design and what a design. You only have to look into the vast array of the heavens to discover what a stunning, incredible and flamboyant artist God is. Did you know that our sun is a star, which is a million times larger than the earth? However, it is only one star in 100 billion stars that make up our galaxy, which is called the Milky Way! The Lord took time and effort to create each star, for each star is different in terms of size, lifetime, colour and temperature. The interesting thing is that our galaxy is only one galaxy in 100 billion galaxies in the universe! Not only that, but our sun is as small as a grain of sand when you compare it to the size of other stars! When the Lord formed the universe, he designed it with thought, flair and effort, all shining out and reflecting his beauty and glory. PSALM 19:1 says, *'The heavens declare the glory of God; the skies proclaim the work of his hands'*.

When the Lord finished creating the world and the universe, he looked at all he had made and said, *"This is good!"*(GEN 1:14-18). But he didn't stop there; he went on to create the birds in the sky, the fish in the seas and animals to live on the land. He didn't just create one type of bird, fish or animal, but as an amazing artist, he created various, wonderful, colourful, extraordinary creatures. There are many television programmes that display and explore the beauty of the many animals, birds and fish that live in this incredible world with us. Scientists will tell you that it is estimated that there are several million species of living things on our planet of which possibly fewer than 10% have been identified. In GENESIS 1:20 the Lord said *"Let the water teem with living creatures"* and this is certainly what happened! No wonder it says in the Bible that as he finished creating the many living creatures he could say, *"This is good!"*

However, he didn't stop there! Then came the best bit of all! He said in GENESIS 1:26, *"Let us make mankind in our image..."*. So then the greatest artist ever shaped, fashioned and formed human beings in his own image. Wow! Just think about this for a moment, not only have we been created, shaped and formed by the greatest, most wonderful, joyful, happy, kind, loving and faithful God but we are also created in his image! Oh how we need a deeper revelation as to who we are for we have been wonderfully made!

You only have to look at the human body to discover God's design is incredible and immensely beautiful. My husband Ray, often says that he can imagine the scene when Adam first sees Eve. God's creation would have been perfect in every way and therefore Ray is sure that Adam's eyes would have bulged with excitement. His heart would have been beating wildly as he saw this incredibly beautiful creature standing beside him and Ray feels that all Adam would have been able to say was *"WOW!"*

Not only did the Lord make mankind immensely beautiful, but he also crafted us with joy and delight. He took so much pleasure in what he had made that when he was finished he didn't just say this is good, this time he said, *"This is very good"*.

We all need to remember this! We have been crafted and formed by the greatest artist ever. His creativity knew no limits as he lovingly shaped his creation. We are his stunning, amazing creation.

Just as the Lord formed Adam and Eve, the Lord has also formed each of us and has sewn beauty, creativity, joy and grace into the fabric of our being. We are beautiful in every way! Wow! The beauty in the universe does not even begin to compare to the beauty that the Lord has poured into you and me! He looks at us every day and with sheer delight and pleasure in his heart he says, *"You are very good!"* His pleasure is not dependant on our colour, shape or size; he loves us from the inside out! He created us with beauty and joy. Even though we live in a fallen state where illness or other physical ailments are present, you remain his choice pearl, his wonderful creation, his joy and his delight!

Oasis of DELIGHT
SPIRITUAL EXERCISES

Paraphrase PSALM 19:1–4A

The heavens declare the glory of God; the skies proclaim the work of his hands. Day after day they pour forth speech; night after night they display knowledge. There is no speech or language where their voice is not heard. Their voice goes out into all the earth, their words to the ends of the world.

Meditate

A number of years ago as a resource, I recorded a meditation CD called 'A God Encounter'. If you have this recording, then play Track 5, which is called 'You are Very Good', if you haven't got that meditation cd, then read through the following meditation and write down what God says to you through it.

You are Very Good
GENESIS 1

Come with me back before time began – when empty darkness covered the face of the earth. The earth was a shapeless, chaotic mess – formless and empty. Breaking into this dark, shapeless, formless mess comes the Word. Like a sharp blade cutting through ice – The Word speaks: *"Let there be light"* and light appears. The light and darkness took it in turns to rule and together they formed the first day. And the Word was delighted and rejoiced in what he had made and said, *"This is good."*

The Word again spoke *"Let the vapours separate to form the sky above and the oceans below."* And it was so – the Word observed what he had made and said, *"This is good"*

The Word spoke to the waters *"Give way. Be gathered into one place and let the earth be seen."* Then the Word spoke to the earth, *"Produce vegetation – trees, grass, plants and fruit of all kinds."* And it happened just as he said. And the Word looked and said, *"This is good."*

The Word spoke *"Let bright lights appear in the sky to give light to the earth and to identify day and night."* The Word made the sun, the moon and the stars to give light on the earth. And the Word was pleased with what he made and said, *"This is good."*

The Word spoke to the waters to produce fish and all kinds of living creatures and it was so. The Word spoke and the skies were filled with birds of every kind. The Word looked at them with pleasure, blessed them and told them *"Multiply – let your numbers increase. Fill the earth."* And the Word said, *"This is good."*

The Word spoke and the land produced every kind of animal, cattle, reptiles, wild creatures, wildlife of every kind. The Word saw what he had made and said, *"This is good."*

The Word then said: *"Let mankind be made in the image of God, rule over the earth, the skies and the seas"*, so the Word created male and female in the image of himself. The Word breathed into mankind the breath of life and blessed them. *"Be fruitful and increase in number, fill the earth, rule over the fish of the seas, the birds of the skies and every living creature that moves."*

The Word looked and danced and rejoiced in what he had made and said, *"This is very good."*

Now, hear the word of God speak deep into your own heart, as God looks at you he says, *"You are very good. You are special in my sight. I have made you in my image and I am pleased with what I have made."* Open up your heart and allow God's word to penetrate your whole being as God says to you *"You are very good"*.

Meditate on PSALM 139:13-14

For you created my inmost being; you knit me together in my mother's womb. I praise you because I am fearfully and wonderfully made; your works are wonderful, I know that full well.

Memorise ACTS 17:28A

For in him we live and move and have our being.

Prayer

Go out for a walk and look for God's creative brush strokes. You may see it in the sky above or in nature around you. As you walk with God, pray and thank him for the wonderful world he has placed us in and for making us his delight!

Thankful Thought

Thank you Lord for being an amazing artist. Thank you that you not only made the heavens and the earth, but you crafted beauty, joy and grace into the fabric of my being. Thank you for making me your choice pearl.

Speak out

I am the Lord's stunning creation!

You are my delight; the apple of my eye

DELIGHT

OUR EXTRAVAGANT GOD

The more you get to know the Lord, the more you recognise that he is an extravagant God. His design of our world and indeed the universe displays his generosity and his creativity. When Jesus was here on earth, he provided food in one instance for 5,000 men besides women and children (probably around 15,000–20,000 people) and in a second instance to 4,000 men and again there would be many more because of women and children. In both these instances, there was more than enough food for everyone plus there was loads left over! Our God is more than generous.

When Simon Peter gave the Lord a loan of his boat so that Jesus could sit in it and preach to the crowds, the Lord showed his outstanding generosity to Peter. It is recorded in LUKE 5:4 that after Jesus had finished teaching, Jesus told him to go into the deep waters and put down his net. As an experienced fisherman, Peter knew that it wasn't the right time of day to fish and also informs Jesus that he and his friends had worked hard all night and caught nothing! However, Peter goes on to say that because Jesus was telling him to do it, he would obey. The Lord met his obedience with an incredible catch. It was so big that the nets began to break and so they signalled to their friends in another boat to come and help. They filled the boats so full that both boats began to sink because of the weight of the catch! Wow! It says that Peter and his companions were astonished at the catch of fish they had taken. Peter had given Jesus the use of his boat not expecting anything in return, but what the Lord did completely overwhelmed him. You can never out give the Lord for our God is so generous!

We should never underestimate the Lord's power or his generosity! When you are in need, when money seems short, when you need an answer, when the impossible raises its head, then remember the power and the generosity of our God and believe that he will provide for you!

A few years ago, my husband and I together with two friends from ngm were praying for a holiday. When Ray asked me where I would like to go, I suggested going to Lincolnshire where I knew there were rented apartments that were big enough to accommodate not only our family, but our friends' family too. However, when I looked on the Internet, I discovered because it was the school half term that the cost was hugely inflated. We noticed that there was only one apartment left to rent and so we prayed not only that we would get this apartment but that we would get it at a reduced price. As we prayed, God told us not to call about the apartment until the day before the school holiday started! It was really difficult to wait until the Friday, but we knew we had heard from God and therefore we just had to be obedient. In any faith walk, it is imperative to keep hearing, obeying and trusting right to the end. I wrote about this important principle in my 'H.O.T. Faith' book. So many times during this walk of faith, the enemy would tell us that when we called on Friday the apartment would be gone! We took all our fears and his lies to God and asked him to keep this apartment for us. On the Friday, I lifted the phone and with my heart beating wildly called the people responsible for the holiday complex. I not only told them that we would like to rent an apartment for the week, but I also asked if they would give us discount considering it was only a day before our holiday dates. They replied that there had been lots of interest in this apartment and they were convinced it would be gone by the end of the day, however they did offer to take a small amount off the bill. I knew this was still far too expensive for us and so I mentioned that on a previous visit I had paid a much less amount for the same apartment. They laughed at the amount

I suggested and said even if they did reduce the price; they would never reduce it by so much! They continued to insist that the apartment would be rented before the day had finished, but on the off chance that it was not, then they would call us by 7pm that evening and discuss it further! Despite the negatives that I had heard, we continued to hold on to God's word and in faith we began to pack our cases! At around 4 o'clock that afternoon, my phone rang and the same woman told me the apartment was still available and asked me this question, *"How much would you like to pay, Mrs Goudie?"* I told her a price that I thought was reasonable and she told me she didn't think I would get it for that price, but would go and check with her superior! They called back a short while later to agree our price! We had the apartment! I gave her my credit card details and paid the holiday in full.

We spent an amazing week in glorious Lincolnshire and the eight of us loved our time away together. At the end of the week, we paid our electricity costs and left thanking God for such a wonderful holiday.

However, God wasn't finished being generous towards us. When I received our credit card statement, our holiday wasn't on it! I called them and explained that although we had stayed in their apartment for a week the money had not been debited from our card. They told me to wait a further month and by then it would definitely be taken. However, in our next month's credit card statement, the bill was still not there. I called again and they assured me that if I had given them the details, then it could take up to three months before showing in our statement. When the situation was still the same after three months, I called again and explained the whole situation once more! After about six or seven phone calls, they eventually said they would look again into my account to check what had happened. They called back to say, *"Mrs Goudie, there is no notification on our system of you ever having stayed at our apartment!"* I told them that we were definitely there and that I had paid the electricity bill at the end of the stay! It was then that they politely but firmly asked me not to call again! I was stunned and when I told a friend of mine about this and asked her what did she think I should do, she said, *"That's wonderful, Nancy, accept it as a gift from the Lord".* It was only then that I could let it go and thank God for his generosity! To be honest, there was nothing else I could do. I had called so many times and in the end I was embarrassed to phone again especially when she had so clearly told me that they didn't want to hear from me!

The amazing thing about this story is that it happened all over again the following year when we booked the same apartment! God's generosity is just amazing! Just recently when I told this story at a conference, a lady told me that the Lord had done the exact same thing for her and her family! Never underestimate what he can do for you! The world might be going through a recession, but our God isn't! He has all the resources you need and above all, never forget how generous he is!

Oasis of DELIGHT
SPIRITUAL EXERCISES

Bible Study - Read JOHN 2:1-11

1. In what way does this tell us about the extravagance of God?

2. Write down any situation in your own life where you have seen the extravagance of God?

3. How does this information help you for the future?

4. Read MATTHEW 20:1-15 – write down what you learn about God's generosity from this passage.

5. Read PSALM 112:5 and write down ways in which you can be generous with your finance, possessions, time etc.

Memorise PHILIPPIANS 4:19

And my God will meet all your needs according to his glorious riches in Christ Jesus.

Meditate on 2 PETER 1:3

His divine power has given us everything we need for life and godliness through our knowledge of him who called us by his own glory and goodness.

Thankful Thought

Thank you Lord for being such a joyful giver. Thank you for all the good things you have given me from the moment I was born until this present day. Thank you too for all you will so generously give me in the future.

Speak out
My needs are all met in you!

The depth of **God's** delight *in us* cannot be measured

DELIGHT

OASIS OF DELIGHT

When the Lord created mankind, he placed Adam and Eve in an oasis called the Garden of Eden. He placed them in a wonderful, beautiful, colourful garden filled with abundant provisions. It was a place of pleasure and sheer delight. In fact the word Eden has two meanings; the first is the word 'delight' and the other is 'pleasure'. One dictionary told me Eden meant 'a place of delight/a state of perfect happiness or bliss'.

God placed his amazing, priceless creation in his delight! Adam and Eve walked in delight, they ran in delight, they lived in delight and were surrounded in every direction by delight. They lived in pleasure, in perfect bliss; in a place of sheer delight. Everything was there for their pleasure! They didn't earn it or even deserve it; they just enjoyed it and walked in it every day! The same is true for you and me! We may not live in the actual Garden of Eden, but God has placed us, his priceless creation, in his delight! He covers us every day with his delight. He causes his delight to fall upon us and he surrounds us with his pleasure. We may not at times feel this is true, but it is indeed the truth! We didn't earn his delight or deserve his grace but every day we walk, run and live in his enormous delight as he pours out his grace so freely upon us. The truth is that we can't go anywhere without his delight and pleasure on us and in us!

It is also true that our amazing God loves us no matter who we are! He does not just love a selected few, but in fact the Bible tells us that he loves the whole world (JOHN 3:16). So even if we choose to live our life without God, he still loves us! Some may never choose to experience what it means to live in an amazing relationship with him, but he still loves them! We are loved delightfully and unconditionally! When you begin to know and experience how much you are loved, it's like walking into a new world that you never knew existed!

Some years ago, one of our ngm team got talking to a girl who worked at that time, in our local superstore. During the course of the conversation the team member invited this girl to come to our ngm church meeting on a Sunday morning. On the day she visited, I got talking to her and she expressed what it was like walking through the gate into the gardens of our ngm Caedmon complex. She told me excitedly, *"It's like walking into*

Narnia! You walk through the superstore car park and though the gate and it's like walking into a completely different world that you didn't know existed; a world full of colour and creativity!" The same is true when we walk into God's garden. It's like walking into a completely different world; a world we perhaps felt only existed for others. It's a world of amazing colour and creativity, full of unconditional love, total acceptance and fullness of joy. When people experience God's delight and realise it is vastly different from the only world they knew, many decide that they cannot live anywhere other than in God's world, in his garden, in his Eden, in his delight!

Oasis of DELIGHT
SPIRITUAL EXERCISES

Paraphrase PSALM 8:3–4

When I consider your heavens, the work of your fingers, the moon and the stars, which you have set in place, what is man that you are mindful of him, the son of man that you care for him?

Memorise PSALM 149:4

For the Lord takes delight in his people; he crowns the humble with salvation.

Meditate on 1 PETER 1:8

Though you have not seen him, you love him; and even though you do not see him now; you believe in him and are filled with an inexpressible and glorious joy, for you are receiving the goal of your faith, the salvation of your souls.

Thankful Thought

Thank you Lord that I am precious in your sight and that I will always find delight and fullness of joy in you.

Speak out

I am placed in your delight; surrounded by your joy and pleasure.

Delight surrounds you constantly

DELIGHT

CREATED WITH DELIGHT
AND FOR PLEASURE!

We were created to live in Eden, in a place of love, joy, peace and pleasure! Adam and Eve were surrounded by pleasure and delight and the Lord wanted them to enjoy the place of bliss that he had created for them both. That's how the Lord wants us to live today! He wants us to enjoy his love, to know what it means to live in delight and to know the sunshine of his pleasure upon our lives. However, the truth is many of us live in fear, worry, concern, insecurity and rejection. Oh, to have our eyes opened to see, feel, know and experience his amazing love, his wonderful delight, his enormous pleasure and his deep, deep, joy in us.

When we first realise that the Lord truly delights in us, the experience changes us forever! When I first realised that God loved me and never ever would reject me, it was a life changing experience. I was only six years of age, but the transformation in me was easily seen! I danced and jumped for joy on my bed! My mum and dad had a really difficult job trying to get me to sleep that night, because I knew something supernatural had happened to me! I had asked God to come into my life and he did! I knew it not just because others told me, or even because the Bible told me, I knew it because I could feel his love and his deep joy burning in my heart!

Not only did I recognise God's delight in me, but also I could not help but express my delight and my joy in him. My heart exploded that night with joy and my six-year-old body could not stop expressing it by dancing on my bed. I may not dance on my bed anymore, (to be honest I don't think the springs could take it!) but the deep delight and joy of knowing God has never left me. ISAIAH 61:10 says, '*I delight greatly in the Lord; my soul rejoices in my God. For he has clothed me with garments of salvation and arrayed me in a robe of righteousness....*' It is because of what Jesus did on the cross two thousand years ago that we can experience a real, joyful, dynamic, powerful life! Oh, the Gospel is such good news! When we begin to understand all that Jesus accomplished, our hearts cannot help but explode with great delight and enormous joy! Have you got joy living in your heart? Have you experienced real delight in the depth of your being? When you do, you just have to let it out! It's impossible to keep such joy locked away. The Gospel is good news to all. It's like finding a huge treasure chest filled with priceless jewels and realising they are all yours

(MATTHEW 13:44)! When we begin to understand that God loves us and delights in us; when it dawns on us that he has given us life to the full (JOHN 10:10), when we truly understand his redemption plan, it's then that we will want to put on our dancing shoes!

When my husband Ray, heard God whisper in his ear one day, *"You are my beloved son in whom I delight"*, it changed him forever. He had struggled for years to know that God really loved him. He had often asked me, *"How can I really know and experience God's love for me?"* However, when he heard the Lord say those words, he was a changed man. He began to know and experience God's love in his inner being and I could see what a difference that had made to Ray. He laughed and cried with joy as the delight of knowing God's love overflowed in his heart. We all so need to hear God's voice telling us how much he loves us!

There is a story that is told of Karl Barth the Swiss Reformed Theologian whom critics say is amongst the most important Christian thinkers of the 20th century. One day at the end of a lecture he was asked what was the greatest thought that had ever gone through his mind. The audience waited with baited breath to hear what one of the greatest minds of the 20th century would give as his answer! After a brief silence and with everyone straining to hear the wisdom that would come from his mouth, he said these words, *"Jesus loves me, this I know, for the Bible tells me so!"* If we really believe the fact that God loves us and that he sent Jesus into the world to show us clearly how much he loves us, this will change our lives forever!

However, hearing that God loves you and experiencing it are two very different things. Although we can hear the words, sometimes we can miss the experience of the reality of those words. Recently, a lady came to my Spiritual Health Weekend worn out from illness and the pressures of life and in need of a touch from the Lord. Before she came she had said to the Lord, *"If you really love me, then please pick me out and give me a gift from Nancy."* At the Spiritual Health Weekends we often through different methods randomly pick people out of the crowd, pray for them and give them a gift. This particular lady had been badly abused in her youth but also during 2011 had many physical things go wrong. She had experienced three very serious asthma attacks, one which ended in the resuscitation room as well as bronchitis, on top of other existing chronic illnesses including diabetes, osteoporosis, bursitis in her hip, both kidneys damaged, clinical depression, an eating disorder and various other medical problems. As well as this, her sister lost twins and her mum got diagnosed with Parkinson's disease! She came to the weekend desperate for a touch from the Lord and that is what she got, in more ways than one.

Right from the beginning of the first meeting, God began to work in this woman's life. She later wrote to say, *"Nancy, normally when I come to your weekends God usually gives me a 'warm up' day on day one, but not this time! He had another plan totally! If I am truly honest, Nancy, I cannot remember a word you preached that first evening, however God used it to reach deep into my soul."* After the session she spoke with Emma, one of the prayer team and kept apologising for her tears. Emma told her there was no need to apologise and began to explain how much God loved her. She told her that she was worthy of God's time and his vast love because of all that Jesus has done on the cross and that made her cry even more! Emma told her that God wanted to give her a gift of a tiara. She said that God wanted to place it on her head to show her that she was his princess! Throughout the weekend, the Lord continued to work in this lady's life by showing her how much he loved her.

At one point as Emma and Zoe (my conference co-ordinator) were praying with her, Zoe felt from the Lord that she should give her a complimentary copy of my book, 'Oasis of Hope'. She smiled and thought, *"Lord, I asked for a gift and here it is! You are amazing!"*

On the last day of the conference she expressed to us that she felt God had done open-heart surgery on her as he revealed the depth and vastness of his love to her. However, God had not yet finished telling her how much he loved her. During one of the sessions, her name was randomly picked out of a basket filled with names. We prayed for her and gave her a special gift never realising that this is what she had asked God to do before she came to the weekend. She thought God had already blessed her with one of my books, but here was God again highlighting her and shining his glory upon her. She said that it was like God was shouting from the rooftops, making sure she had heard that he REALLY, REALLY loved her!

Your name might never have been picked out of a basket, but today God wants you to know that he really, really loves you. He hasn't forgotten you! He never will leave you nor will he ever forsake you! He won't fail you ever! Don't just listen to the teaching in this book that tells you that God delights in you, but instead ask him to show you how much he loves you and I have no doubt that through various ways he will do so.

Today, find time to sit and listen to the voice of God; listen to his words of delight and joy! Ask him what he thinks of you! Ask his Holy Spirit to drench you with his love and joy. When we hear his voice and his words of divine pleasure in us, our prospective of life will change forever. You might find yourself so full of his Spirit and so full of his joy that you can't stop laughing! The Gospel is so amazing!

Oasis of DELIGHT
SPIRITUAL EXERCISES

Answer the following questions:

> **1.** How can we get to know God's delight in us?

> **2.** What would stop you from enjoying God's enormous pleasures?

> **3.** Read PSALM 37:4 and write down what this verse says to you.

Read EPHESIANS 3: 16–19 and insert your name in the verses making it personal to you.

Prayer

Ask the Lord this question: *"What do you think of me, Lord?"* Then write down his answer. Spend some time thanking him for his love for you and that the Gospel is such good news!

Meditate on a piece of chocolate. Use your senses (sight, smell, touch, taste and hearing) to meditate on a small piece of chocolate (or if you don't like chocolate perhaps use a mint) and ask God to speak to you through it about his love for you.

Paraphrase Isaiah 61:10A

I delight greatly in the Lord; my soul rejoices in my God. For he has clothed me with garments of salvation and arrayed me in a robe of righteousness.

Thankful Thought

Thank you Lord for your wonderful love for me! Thank you that you continually pour your love and grace upon me and devise ways of letting me know just how much you love me!

Speak out
I am not only loved and accepted, but I am God's delight and his immense pleasure!

You are my **chosen one**; the one in whom I take **great delight**

DELIGHT

GOD SEES THE BEAUTY IN US!

When the Lord placed Adam and Eve in the Garden of Eden, he did not leave them alone and disappear from view! It tells me in GENESIS 3 that God walked with them in the garden. He loved his relationship with them. The Lord did not create human beings because he was lonely or felt the need for companionship, but he made us because he wanted to do so! Ray and I didn't have children because we wanted them to provide for us in our old age. We wanted children so that we could pour our love upon them and be with them. When they were born, we couldn't help but demonstrate our deep delight in them by hugging and kissing them constantly. We may not hug and kiss them as much as we did then (not sure they would like us to do that in front of their mates) but we do continue to pour our love on them and want the very best for them. We have loved every stage of their lives and love the intimacy we have with them. Similarly, the Lord wants a deep and close relationship with his creation; he wants to walk with us every day and show by his love just how much he takes pleasure in us!

When I tell people that God delights in them, many find it difficult to accept that God could possibly see something of value in them! Often this is because of guilt or shame or even because they have a wrong view of themselves or of God. I read recently the story of how Michelangelo had crafted his masterpiece, the statue of David, from a piece of castaway marble. The marble was so ruined that it was deemed to be of no value at all by other artists. However, when Michelangelo saw that piece of marble, instead of seeing a ruined piece of marble, he saw what no one else could see. He saw shape, texture and beauty in what others had thrown away! Michelangelo once said that his job as an artist was to release David from the stone and that is what he did! God sees the beauty in each of us! He sees potential where others see failure! He sees someone of immense value and every day whether you experience it or not, he pours his delight into you.

I once told a mother that her daughter was a beautiful girl both inside and out! Her daughter looked like a model and had a very kind and generous spirit. A few days later her daughter told me that when I left, her mother said to her, *"What does Nancy see in you that I don't?"*

God always sees the beauty in us and sings with delight over us. It doesn't matter who we are, what country we were born in, what colour our skin is, what shape or size we are, what intelligence we display, the Lord loves us all and delights in the diversity of his creation. It doesn't even matter what you have done, God simply and unconditionally loves you. The deepest desire in his heart is to have an amazing relationship with you. No matter how many times you have been intentionally or unintentionally rejected or hurt by others, the truth is you are valued and loved by our amazing God!

I know what it's like to be deeply hurt and rejected and it doesn't get easier the more it happens. Someone speaks badly of you, another refuses to speak to you, someone else spreads false rumours to many of your friends, another spits damaging words out in anger and pain fills your heart. It's not easy when you are on the receiving end of rejection. The saying goes, 'Sticks and stones may break my bones, but words will never hurt me', but it's not true! Words can often damage us even more deeply than someone physically hitting us! I want you to know that the Lord will never do this to you! Trust him and allow his tender words to bring healing to your heart.

Spiritual Exercises

Memorise 1 JOHN 3:1A

How great is the love the Father has lavished on us, that we should be called children of God! And that is what we are!

Meditate on 1 JOHN 4:9

This is how God showed his love among us: He sent his one and only Son into the world that we might live through him.

Paraphrase PSALM 36:7

How priceless is your unfailing love! Both high and low among men find refuge in the shadow of your wings.

Thankful Thought

Thank you that you love me and always believe in me.

Speak out

My trust is in your unfailing love!

Delight **lights up the soul** and lets the **sun shine**

DELIGHT

THE ABUSER WAS ONLY
GIVEN A SLAP ON THE WRIST

Nancy Hall had always had a difficult relationship with her mum. She told me it all started when her grandmother's boyfriend sexually abused her. When she finally plucked up the courage to tell her mum, she was told that she didn't believe her and to stop being an attention seeker. So she kept the abuse and the pain of what was happening locked securely within her! Two years later her sister made the same revelation to her mum and it was only then that her mum realised that it must be true. However even then, her mum didn't go to the police but just gave the abuser a slap on the wrist.

She was 13 when the abuse started and it didn't stop until three long, hard years had gone by. On top of this, Nancy found it very difficult to make friends as throughout her young life she had been bullied. At the age of 16 her parents split up due to her mum's heavy drinking and both her and her sister were given the choice of which parent they wanted to live with. Her sister chose her mum and

Nancy chose to live with her dad and his partner. However, a couple of months later her world fell apart once more when her dad fell out of the window of their third floor flat and died. She then had to go back to live with her mum, but a couple of weeks later she ran away to live once more with her step mum. However, this arrangement didn't work for long because without her Dad, she didn't feel part of her step mum's family anymore. So she had to go back to her mum's house. At the age of 19 she left her family and her native Belgium and came to live in England.

Many years later, she was sitting in my Spiritual Health Weekend when a guest speaker called Carl Wills, picked her out and prophesied over her. He said, amongst other things that throughout her life the Lord had always been her friend, but that he wanted her to know that this was especially true during the ages of 13, 14, 15, 16 and 17. Carl had no idea what had happened to Nancy during that time of her life, but the words he spoke brought such healing to her. The Lord wanted her to know that when she was at her lowest, he never once left her!

I believe too that there will be people reading this book who need to hear that during the darkest times of your life, the Lord has never left you! He is not an abuser! He is the most faithful, loving and kind dad you could ever have. He never leaves you to walk through dark valleys on your own. The truth is that through those painful, hard journeys he, in actual fact, carries you in his arms. Healing, freedom and joy are given as part of our inheritance and the great news is they are only a prayer away!

SPIRITUAL EXERCISES

Meditate on DEUTERONOMY 33:27A

The eternal God is your refuge, and underneath are the everlasting arms.

Memorise ISAIAH 40:8

The grass withers and the flowers fall, but the word of our God stands forever.

Paraphrase ISAIAH 40: 28-31

Do you not know? Have you not heard? The Lord is the everlasting God, the Creator of the ends of the earth. He will not grow tired or weary, and his understanding no one can fathom. He gives strength to the weary, and increases the power of the weak.

Even youths grow tired and weary and young men stumble and fall; but those who hope in the Lord will renew their strength. They will soar on wings like eagles; they will run and not grow weary, they will walk and not be faint.

Thankful Thought

Thank you that even in the very tough times of life, you never leave me not even for a split second! What an amazing dad you are!

Speak out

I am safe in God's arms!

Experience **real love**
and you will **never**
run out of delight

DELIGHT

THE LORD HAS TIME FOR EACH OF US!

Ray and I received a beautiful heartfelt letter recently from a girl called Shona, who had been in ngm for the last two years. One of the things she said in the letter is that she wanted to thank us for our input into her life. She said she had left her native Scotland for a year thinking she would just take a year out of her teaching job to have some fun with dancing before going back to the world of teaching. However, what happened was that in the time she was here, so many of her heart desires and dreams were fulfilled. She received dance training of a very high standard during her time at ngm and we were all thrilled when she secured a job as a dancer in the popular show, 'High School Musical'. Throughout her time at ngm she had also grown spiritually and her relationship with the Lord had deepened enormously.

Both Ray and I just love seeing what God does in people who come to ngm. The difference from when they arrive to when they leave is just wonderful! We love to find out people's deep desires and passions and help them in any way we can to see those passions fulfilled. Shona was important to us, as is everyone who comes into ngm and therefore our leaders and ourselves invest our time and our hearts into them so that we can see them grow to their fullest potential.

The wonderful thing about the Lord is that he has time for every single one of us and he wants us to see our visions and desires succeed. PSALM 37:4 says, *'Delight yourself in the Lord and he will give you the desires of your heart'*. It's never a chore to spend time with Jesus; it's always an adventure as you never know what he is going to say or do. When I have read my Bible out of habit or out of duty, then it can become a chore, but when I read it with the Holy Spirit, having faith in my heart and expecting him to speak to me, it is dynamite! Our God is incredible; he is full of joy, fun, wisdom and power and therefore it's such an adventure and a real delight to spend quality time with him.

Just recently a lady wrote to me to tell me about a revelation she recently received whilst spending time with the Lord. She awoke one morning to discover that her house and the area around her home had a power cut and therefore she could not do all she had originally planned to do that particular day. As it was raining outside she felt she couldn't go for a walk and so she decided to go back to bed and spend some time with her Heavenly Father. As she closed her eyes, she immediately saw a vision of the Lord sitting on a fallen tree, so in her imagination she sat at his feet and laid her head on his lap. He began to stroke her hair and with each stroke it seemed as though the hard times she had been experiencing in life were being soaked with his peace. During this time she began to realise that she was alone with the Lord and that he had quality time to spend with her. It dawned on her for the first time that there must be a massive amount of people spending time with him, but even though the demand on his time must be enormous, here he was sitting with her and not in a hurry! It was just her and her Heavenly Dad spending a peaceful time together. Just as the Lord had time for Adam and Eve, the Lord has time for each of us. He is with us constantly and has time to listen to all our deepest cries. The Bible tells us that he is Omni-present, which means he can be everywhere at once and therefore does not need to be looking over his shoulder wondering if he is late for his next appointment. He has quality time for each one of us! So go on, spend some time in his presence. Sit at his feet and rest your head on his lap. His enormous desire is for you to discover and enjoy all the many and wonderful pleasures that are found in him.

SPIRITUAL EXERCISES

Meditate on PSALM 31:15A

My times are in your hands.

Bible Study - Read MATTHEW 19:13-15

1. In the days when Jesus was alive, the culture said that women and children were not important. What does this passage tell us about how Jesus treated little children?

2. Jesus had a busy schedule, yet he had time for little children. Where else in the Bible does it show that Jesus had time for others? (e.g. see LUKE 18:35-43; LUKE 19:1-6; JOHN 13:1-15; JOHN 19:25-27)

3. No matter who you are the Lord Jesus has time for you – write down how that makes you feel.

4. When is the last time you selflessly gave of your time to someone else not expecting anything back in return?

5. Write down something you can pledge to do for someone else and make sure you do it within a short period of time. It can be something really simple, like sending a card or buying them a box of chocolates.

Memorise JOHN 6:37B

Whoever comes to me I will never drive away!

Thankful Thought

Thank you Lord that I am important to you and that you always have time for me! Thank you that you have an adventure full of pleasures for me.

Speak out

I am valuable and I am loved.

It's **sheer delight** to sit in **God's shade**

DELIGHT

CULTIVATE HIS DELIGHT

When the Lord placed Adam in the Garden of Eden, as well as giving him the garden to enjoy, he also gave him the responsibility of taking care of the garden (GENESIS 2:15). It's important also for us to take care of the place God has brought us to so that we cultivate his delight and his pleasure in our hearts. Once we realise that God loves us and we take the step of asking him into our lives, it is then important to cultivate our relationship with him. In order for a relationship to develop, as it should between two people, it needs both persons to be active in making it happen.

If I were to become one of your friends, then I would need to make sure I spent time with you. I would ask you questions and I would answer your questions. I would find out about your background, your family and your experiences. I would want to know your thoughts, your hopes, your dreams and I would share mine with you! I wouldn't spend time with you because I have to, but I would spend time with you because I want to. That is what friendship is all about. The same is true with the Lord. In order to get to really know the Lord, we need to spend time with him, but we don't spend time with him as a duty, rather we linger in his presence because spending time with him is so pleasurable! If your time with God is not a pleasure, then dare I suggest that perhaps you have never really known him? To know him and to walk with him means that similar to the disciples on the road to Emmaus, our hearts will burn within us with excitement and immense joy (LUKE 24:32). When Jesus spoke with the woman at the well, he told her, *"If you knew the gift of God and who it is that asks you for a drink, you would have asked him and he would have given you living water"* (JOHN 4:10). It's living water he wants to give us, not old, stale, stagnant, boring water. It's joy everlasting! He wants to give us pleasures forevermore. If we really know Jesus and the pleasures he can give us, then we would be running into his presence! Oh we so need to know him in this way! The more we get to know Jesus, the more we realise he is not like the picture sometimes painted of him. He is not an angry God ready to hit you over the head with a big black Bible every time you do something wrong! He is indeed the God of joy and pleasure and therefore it is fun, exciting and such an adventure to share our lives with him.

Many people ask me for prayer because their spiritual life is struggling, but when I ask them how much time they spend alone with Jesus, I discover that they spend very little or no time at all. When will we begin to understand that he is the source of unending pleasure? PSALM 16:11 says, *'In your presence there is fullness of joy; at your right hand are pleasures forevermore'* (English Standard Version). Come on - let's be a pleasure seeker! Let's hang around the source of all joy and let his wonderful fragrance fill our lives. There is such joy in knowing Jesus. That's not to say that every day is a laugh a minute; sometimes life can be very hard and difficult, however, even in those difficult times because Jesus is with us we can find real joy in his presence!

A number of years ago, I made a conscious decision to get up even earlier in the morning and spend quality time with the Lord. I was on holiday at the time and so before anyone else was awake, I went and sat at the pool and read my Bible. No one else was there apart from the pool attendants who were cleaning the chairs and tidying up the pool area. Each day as I sat reading, praying and studying God's written word, the presence of God would come down upon me! Two hours later, I had to drag myself away to go to breakfast with the others; my time with Jesus seemed far too short. Each day, my heart would be filled so full that I was ready to explode with joy and delight! When I came home from holiday, I made sure that my alarm was set early in the morning in order for me to have quality time with Jesus before having to get myself and my family ready for the day ahead. I still do this today!

This decision often means that I have to go to bed early but if you want a dynamic relationship with the Lord, you will be prepared to do anything to make it happen! I remember hearing about a young guy who travelled vast distances at the weekend just to spend a few hours with his girlfriend. It cost him lots in terms of finance, time and other relationships, but none of these things seemed to matter to him as long as he spent time with the girl of his dreams. If we want something bad enough, we will choose to sacrifice other things in order to make it happen.

When Ray and I responded to the call of God on our lives to leave our home, our car, our families, our friends, our church and our jobs in Ayr in Scotland and travel to Wolverhampton in England the sacrifice seemed so small. We left a beautiful seaside resort in Ayr, our three bedroomed bungalow, our sporty car (the car came with Ray's job) and two very good jobs to work with British Youth for Christ. We didn't know anyone in Wolverhampton apart from two dear friends whom we had got to know the previous year and so they invited Ray and I to live with them. They lived in a BYFC house, which they rented in the red light district of Wolverhampton. The house had dampness running down some of its walls and prostitutes touting for business outside, yet we never looked back once because we were so excited at the journey God had us on. As the years passed, people would often ask us about the sacrifice we had made, but it didn't even occur to us that it was a sacrifice! We had fallen in love with Jesus and we only wanted to do what he wanted us to do no matter where that was or what that entailed! Knowing all the ups and downs, the good and the not so good times, the pain and the hardships we have been through since our call in 1980, the question is, would we do it all again? The answer is a resounding YES! There is such fun, adventure, laughter, joy and delight in getting to know God and following his will for our lives which far outweighs the painful and hard times that we often experience. Let me remind you again that the Gospel is such good news!

The amazing truth is that the more you get to know the Lord, the more you realise that there is so much more to know! Even though Paul had incredible heavenly visions, even though he was caught up into paradise and heard things he was not permitted to tell others, he still poured out a cry from his heart, *"I want to know Christ."* We will never get to the end of knowing all there is to know but the more you do know, the more you want to know! The more you experience his delight and his joy, the more you find you cannot live without really knowing him. There is no other way of knowing the Lord, other than spending time with him. I know how easy it is for our attention to be taken up with the worries and cares that this world brings, but if we don't tend the garden so to speak, the weeds will grow so quickly and begin to squeeze the joy, laughter and delight out of your heart.

When someone doesn't spend time with the Lord his or her spiritual light within dulls and they can easily fall away! Falling away from God never happens overnight, it's always a process. If you stop spending time alone with him, you will find that the temptation to do wrong seems to burn more strongly within you! However, when you spend time with the Lord and keep his word in your heart, then when temptation comes you can fight it much more easily. Experiencing Jesus and his joy is the best antidote ever to sinning!

I love the fact that when you cultivate your relationship with him, he can speak at any time and tell you to do something that will change someone's life. One day, I was sorting out my mail at my computer and saw a letter from a lady who had initially contacted me by telephone asking for prayer. I felt a little nudge to contact this lady again and there and then wrote a little note and felt from the Lord I should include a copy of my book, 'Oasis of Hope'. I did what I felt the Lord wanted me to do and prayed that the note and the book would encourage her. Some weeks later I got a letter back from her to tell me that the day my book and note arrived was the day after she had seen a close friend die! She had been reeling from this death and was finding it difficult to have any hope for the future, when on her doorstep arrived my encouraging note and a book containing wonderful stories of hope! As she read the book, the stories filled her heart with real dynamic hope. She wrote to me and said, *"You have no idea what a blessing this has been at just the right time. When your letter arrived a friend of mine had just died. I had sat watching her slowly slip away to the Lord the previous day and because of other negative stuff happening in my life, I was really floundering in a place of despair and hopelessness. This precious book has been a literal GODSEND!"*

She started to do the spiritual exercises at the end of every chapter and was finding that the exercises were encouraging her and bringing her much needed refreshment. On the back of the card she sent to me was the printed words 'Blank Inside' to which she had put a little note that said, *"Not any more!"*

When you spend time with Jesus and dwell in his presence you can't help but know more of how much he loves and delights in you! When you begin to believe that truth, your life will never be the same again! Smith Wigglesworth, a powerful man of God who used to live many years ago said, *"If we only knew how precious we were in the sight of God, we would scarcely be able to sleep for thinking of his watchful loving care. There is nothing like it."* It is so true; there is nothing in this world that comes even close to the thrill of knowing how much God delights in each of us. Let's remember to keep cultivating our relationship with him and keep tending the garden of our lives to make sure that the weeds are never given an opportunity to grow!

SPIRITUAL EXERCISES

Meditate on this phrase from PHILIPPIANS 3:10

I want to know Christ.

Memorise 1 JOHN 4:19

We love because he first loved us.

Write a Psalm

Write a psalm to God telling him of your heart to know him better. Tell him how much you love him because of all he has done for you!

Thankful Thought

Thank you that you extortionately love me despite all my faults.

Speak out

I am a pleasure seeker; I sit at God's right hand where there are pleasures forevermore.

Drink from the
river of delights

DELIGHT

LISTENING TO THE TRUTH

I heard a story recently of what happened to Fred Astaire, the greatest known dancer in the world, when he was attending an audition to get a job before he was famous! After his audition, the Director of the show wrote the following words on his report on Fred, *'can't sing, can't act, can dance a little!'* We can laugh at this now knowing that Fred went on to be one of the most amazing singers, actors and exceptional dancers of his time, but I am sure those words must have hurt. However, despite the negative comments, Fred went on to prove his critic wrong!

I was walking down a street with a group of friends in Spain one day, when one of them said in my hearing, *"The only thing Nancy has going for her is her boobs!"* When the others chastised her for her words, she went on to explain that in her opinion I would look nothing without the shape of my boobs! I laughed at what she said with the others in the group, but later thought to myself that if I had been insecure those words could have deeply hurt me. I had gone through years of hearing Ray tell me that he thought I was beautiful (even though he sees me at my worst!) and therefore her words didn't hurt as much as they would have if I hadn't known the deep love of my husband. When we know that God delights in us, when we really know that he loves us warts and all, then we can deal with the criticisms that life often brings. His love and his delight will strengthen our inner being and keep us from despair.

The way to hear his voice is to keep reading the Bible and sit in his presence daily. When we soak ourselves in him and his word, when we listen to the truth and hide it deep within us, then we will experience how the truth can set us free from the lies the enemy can fool us into believing. Do remember it was the lies of the serpent in the garden that eventually led to sin and fear instead of revelling in joy and delight.

Recently I heard a story of an 80-year-old man who had felt he had 'lost' his salvation. He was so disturbed that all he could do was to cry at the top of his voice, *"I am lost! I am lost!"* His wife took him to Smith Wigglesworth's house to ask if Smith would pray for him. When Smith arrived home it was impossible not to hear the utter despair in this man's voice as he shouted at the top of his voice, *"I am lost! I have committed the unpardonable sin. I am lost. I am lost!"* When I heard this story, I was already thinking in my mind what I would do or say to change this man's condition, however what Smith Wigglesworth did didn't occur to me at the time! Led by the Holy Spirit, Smith Wigglesworth commanded the lying spirit to come out! In a moment, the evil spirit left and the man was completely free! What a lesson for us all. We must not allow the lies of the enemy to find a place in our lives. The devil knows that if he can capture our thought life, he has won a mighty victory over us!

Jesus tells us that when the devil lies he speaks his native language, for he is a liar and is the father of lies (JOHN 8:44) yet when he whispers in our ear that we are useless and unloved, we automatically believe him. The Bible, which is the word of God, is full of how much God loves each of us. 1 JOHN 3:1 exclaims, *'How great is the love the Father has lavished on us....'* Wow! He has lavished his love upon each of us. It's not just a small amount; it is an outstanding amount, so much so that we can never calculate the measurements of the depth, length, breadth and height of the love of God (EPHESIANS 3:16-19). The truth is that the Lord loves each of us so completely and so wonderfully that if we truly knew how much he loved us we would all be so overwhelmed. What often happens though is that we believe the lies we tell ourselves or that others have told us and therefore find it so hard to enter into all that God wants us to experience.

Joanna, her mum and her sister booked in March 2011 to come to my 2012 Spiritual Health Weekend. At that time Joanna was living with her boyfriend, however because the relationship they had was very unhealthy they broke up in the September of that year. At the lowest point in their relationship, Joanna prayed that God would somehow remove her from her unsafe situation and put her where he wanted her to be. Within one week of that prayer, she was living in an affordable, comfortable, safe apartment ten minutes away from her sister and attending an Alpha course! Through that time, God transformed her and her outlook on life, however there was always one heavy stone left in her heart that was hard to heal and that was her relationship with her mum.

Her entrance into the world was very traumatic and it resulted in her mum being in a coma for the first part of her life. Because of this and also her mum then having severe postnatal depression (puerperal psychosis), she was mostly cared for by her dad, her grandma and also her siblings and therefore did not feel as though she had bonded with her mother. When she was growing up, she held on to feelings of abandonment and therefore began to reject her

mother's love. As Joanna grew into an adult she
could see that her mum was a loving, kind, strong
and wonderful person, but still she could not feel
any love towards her. She carried a lot of guilt, pain,
resentment and bitterness around within her and
although she knew that carrying all this pain was
unnecessary, she could not shift it. So instead of
dealing with it, she squashed it deep inside herself
and tried as best she could to ignore it.

Just before coming to my Spiritual Health Weekend
she prayed and asked the Lord to change the
situation and help her to grow a deep love for her
mum. She had no idea how this would happen but
put the request into the hands of Jesus.

On the first evening, she felt the Lord take a hold
of the hard stone within her heart and place his
jewels within it. She would have loved to have
prayed with her mum, but knew she couldn't tell
her mum that although she acted loving and kind
towards her, actually she could feel no bond of love
between them at all. So she said to the Lord, *"I am
so happy you have now taken the pain away in my
heart, but please Lord help me to begin to feel love for
my mum."*

On the late Saturday afternoon session, I always
have a word from God for everyone who attends

the weekends. This is something I have done for many years. I take time throughout the year to pray for those who have booked in and ask God to give me something that he wants to say to them. When Joanna and her mum went to receive their words because their surname was the same, they were standing next to each other. As the word was read over Joanna, it was like a floodgate opened in her heart and a huge torrent of water burst through. She could not control the tears. Joanna picked up courage and asked the question that she had longed to ask for many years. With tears running down her face she said to her mum, *"Did you resent me when I was born?"* Her mother answered truthfully, *"No"* and then kept repeating *'No'* many times. Joanna told me that with every *'No'* something inside her melted! Her mum went on to say, *"I was just so relieved that you were normal and healthy."* When they hugged Joanna knew all the fears and lies she had held on to for many years were gone.

Are you listening to the truth or are you allowing the enemy's lies to blind you? How can we guard against this? We can soak ourselves in the truth of the word of God and use the weapons of warfare that the Lord has so graciously given us. These spiritual weapons have divine power to demolish every lie, argument or false thought we might have and make each one obedient to Jesus (2 CORINTHIANS

10:4-5). Let's not allow the enemy to fool us any longer. The word of God is living and active, sharper than any double-edged sword; so let it cut through the rubbish and clutter we often keep in our hearts and minds. Keep soaking yourself every day in God's word. Drink in the truth through reading, meditating and memorising scripture. I wonder how many lies of the enemy we entertain in our hearts and in our minds, rather than commanding the lying spirit to leave in the name of our precious Lord Jesus! Let's fill our minds with the truth and allow the truth of a happy, loving, kind and faithful God to set us free. Let's only allow the word of God to shape us and therefore make us into the people we were created to be.

Keep being drenched in the Holy Spirit until you are so full you overflow in the Spirit. Let the truth find a resting place in your heart until you are no longer just reading words, but you believe every word that comes from the mouth of God. Pursue him and his truth always and the difference will be seen in you! When we find out who God made us to be, we will never want to be anyone else because God made each of us so perfectly and so wonderfully! He made you and me his delight! Wow!

SPIRITUAL EXERCISES

Meditate on JOHN 8:32

Then you will know the truth, and the truth will set you free.

Write a prayer to God thanking him for his truth and asking him to help you to not only know his truth but also discern and reject the lies that come from the enemy. (Do remember that Jesus called the devil, the father of all lies – see JOHN 8:44)

Memorise MATTHEW 4:4

Man does not live on bread alone, but on every word that comes from the mouth of God.

Meditate on a cupcake (or something similar)

Use your senses (sight, smell, touch, taste and hearing) to meditate on a cupcake or something similar and ask God to speak to you through it. Write down what he says.

Paraphrase PROVERBS 30:5

Every word of God is flawless; he is a shield to those who take refuge in him.

Thankful Thought

Thank you that your truth sets me free and brings healing to my heart.

Speak Out

I am always loved and accepted by the eternal, loving, kind and faithful God.

To **know his delight**
will keep you **climbing**
any mountains you
face in life

DELIGHT

THE LORD SINGS OVER YOU!

uring the writing of this book, I personally had an amazing revelation of God's delight. In ZEPHANIAH 3:17 it says, *'The Lord your God is with you, he is mighty to save. He will take great delight in you, he will quiet you with his love, he will rejoice over you with singing'*. This has always been a very special verse for me and I have always enjoyed reading and meditating on it. However, one day in the early hours of the morning, God brought the reality of this verse home to me. I don't know whether I was asleep or awake, I don't know whether I was genuinely hearing this or in the Spirit, but I know it was real. I heard the sound of God singing over us, his creation and it was incredible. The sound was loud, but gentle, it was melodic and tuneful, it was filled with harmonies even though it was only one voice. The song was saturated with the greatest joy I have ever known and on hearing the sound it made me want to explode with joy. It was bursting with creativity and God's enormous pleasure was within every note. The sound of his voice didn't just fill my mind; it seemed to me that even the whole universe was not big enough to contain this most amazing voice. I had never heard such stunning singing; it was truly not of this world. As I was listening to God's song, the Lord spoke to my heart and said, *"Nancy, I constantly sing songs of delight and joy over you; I sing like this over everyone!"* I knew from the Bible that the Lord sings over us, but now I had heard the beautiful sound of his voice for myself. It was genuinely incredible; words cannot even begin to describe it, no adjectives I could use would do it justice! It was a sound that I wanted to listen to forever.

When Ray goes into the studio to record a song, he will often tell the singer to make the lyrics bleed. What he means by this is for the singer to really live the lyrics and allow their emotions to be released through the song. He wants them to feel what they are singing and to tell the story with deep passion. When I heard the Lord's song, the thought that occurred to me was that if Ray had been producing the sound, he wouldn't have needed to tell the Lord to show emotion or passion it was already there in huge quantities. His voice was full of emotion and his passion was so strong. His love, his grace and his heart for each of us came across so clearly. He bleeds delight into every note and the sound he makes reaches the depth of your being.

In some way it reminded me of the stories in Greek mythology, where dangerous female creatures used to sing the most beautiful of songs and lure nearby sailors with their enchanting voices so that they ended up shipwrecked on the rocky coast of an island. The sound of their voices was so amazing that it hypnotised them to their fateful death. The sound I heard was so beautiful that I could not help but be drawn and attracted to the one who sings such songs of love and delight. The main difference was that it did not lead to death but to life in all its colour and fullness.

Come and listen to his song of joy over you! You may not have the same experience as me, but my prayer will be that as you meditate on the word of God and allow it to take root within you, you will know that he is constantly singing songs of delight over you! His song is the most beautiful thing you could ever hear. Tune into Heaven's sounds today and listen to the greatest symphony ever.

SPIRITUAL EXERCISES

Meditate on ZEPHANIAH 3:17

*The Lord your God is with you, he is mighty to save.
He will take great delight in you, he will quiet you
with his love, he will rejoice over you with singing.*

Bible Study

It is interesting to note that singing is mentioned
many times in the Bible. Look up the following
references to find out how God and others use
singing in the Bible:

> **1.** PSALM 68:6
> **2.** 2 CHRONICLES 20:1-30
> **3.** ACTS 16:16-40
> **4.** PSALM 13:6
> **5.** EPHESIANS 5:18-20
> **6.** 1 CORINTHIANS 14:13-15
> **7.** PSALM 59:16

Prayer

The Lord loves to hear us sing, so whether you consider yourself to be a singer or not, take time to sing a song of joy to the Lord and then listen to his reply to you.

Thankful Thought

Thank you Lord for taking great delight in me and for rejoicing over me with singing.

Speak out

I am always surrounded by the melody of God's delight.

Delight is shown in a smile or in a song

DELIGHT

THE GIFT OF SEX

When the Lord placed Adam and Eve into his garden (or oasis) of delight, he also gave them gifts to enjoy. One of the gifts he gave to them was the gift of sex.

During the 1980's Ray and I travelled around the UK and beyond with the band we founded called 'Heartbeat'. Just before one of our visits to a town in the UK, one of the organisers asked if we would speak to a school's Christian Union on the subject of sex. Ray almost collapsed when I told him that I had volunteered him to deliver the talk! However, despite the daunting task, Ray prepared a talk to Christians on how to keep ourselves pure in a world where sex is openly flaunted as a commodity at us from every angle. Television adverts to promote cars, or drinks or even antiperspirants nearly always seem to contain a near naked girl.

We thought there would be around 10–15 people attending the seminar, however when we arrived at the school premises, Ray was shocked to discover that the seminar and its subject had been advertised to the whole school. There were posters everywhere! When we arrived at the venue, not only was the place packed full of students, but also we noticed that the posters had enticed some of the teachers to attend. The subject of sex had attracted hundreds of teenagers and most of them were not Christians!

By this time, Ray was in a panic! He had prepared a talk that was totally unsuitable for the large audience that had turned up! So he tore up his notes and said a quick prayer! He then opened his seminar with the following statement! *"I believe Christians are the sexiest people on the planet!"* Every eye was on Ray as he unpacked that statement and told everyone that the God that we knew and loved had created sex for our pleasure. I am sure the Christians in the building were wondering where Ray was going with this statement and the people who were not yet Christians were thinking, *"Hey, this man is speaking my language!"* Ray then began to tell them that if God created sex then he would know the best way to use this gift. The creator always knows the best way to enjoy his creation. He went on to explain how God wants the pleasure of sex to be enjoyed to the full within a loving, caring marriage. He had everyone in the place spellbound, not that they all agreed with everything he said, but it gave them much to think about. We would have loved to listen in to their private conversations afterwards, particularly the ones in the staff room!

In the church culture I grew up in, sex was never talked about as a gift from God! It was as though God himself, never mind the church leaders were embarrassed about sex. There was a clear message from everyone around me that sex was something to be avoided at all costs. When someone got pregnant without being married, the person was rejected from the church and talked about in negative terms. In my mind and I'm sure in many others too, it became something dirty rather than a precious gift from God. There is such a need today to speak about sex as it really is: a good and perfect gift from God, given to us for our pleasure (JAMES 1:17).

My husband Ray often tells a story about a man who spoke at a wedding and within his talk mentioned that it was God who created the orgasm. The best man, who was not a Christian, could not believe what he had just heard and so asked, *"Do you mean to tell me that the God you are talking about is the God who made the orgasm, the most incredible pleasure known to mankind? Now if that is true, then that is the kind of God I could believe in!"*

Obviously God has given us clear boundaries to his precious gift and when it is used in the context of marriage, it is an amazing gift. Rather than God being embarrassed about sex, he delights in this gift! He has given us a good and wonderful gift and as the church we need to be much more open and informative about this gift. It would be wonderful to hear the church talk more positively about sex and its proper place in our lives.

Sexual intercourse, of course, is not just a physical union, it is an emotional, spiritual and psychological union too and often people don't understand this and get hurt through casual sex. I have spoken and prayed with many people who have been hurt and damaged by using this precious gift in the wrong way. Many look for real love and then realise that all they received was a damaging sexual experience. Emma was one of these people and she recently shared her story with me!

Although a big part of Emma's childhood was attending church every Sunday surrounded by people with a really strong faith in God and although God was always real to her, she never allowed him to come close.

When she began secondary school her mind was set on fitting in with the rest of the class. The fact that her parents were Christians who went to church was embarrassing and therefore it was a subject that she would never discuss with her peers. She felt ashamed that she didn't belong to a 'normal' family and at that point began to reject all she had been taught in her early years. She had always been a very independent girl and so she made up her mind to leave Jesus behind as she pursued all that life had to offer. She deliberately chose to close her heart to the Lord and she told me it was that decision that set her on a pathway to deep pain.

She had a huge need within her to be loved and accepted but instead of turning to the one who could help, she turned to the boys around her. There was a huge void within her and she tried to fill that vast emptiness with many boy relationships! Some relationships were more serious than others, but all of them left painful deep wounds within her. As Emma's self worth was so low, she would strive harder and harder for that perfect relationship that would fill the void. It wasn't long before she was giving to the boys what they wanted - sexual pleasure, but with every experience her heart would be broken again and again.

Whilst a young teenager, she and her family discovered that her Dad had cancer. This was a huge shock to everyone in the family and it really rocked Emma. In an attempt to protect her already damaged heart, she closed herself off even more from her parents and from God and allowed sex to be a substitute for love. Although she had an incredible need for real, dynamic love, she found herself pushing her Dad away during his illness. One thing she couldn't understand, however, was that although her Dad had been diagnosed with cancer, it didn't seem to knock her parents' faith. In fact their faith appeared to be stronger than ever! Their faith was such an example to many especially when her dad died two years later. She now knows that it was because of their great example that she didn't blame God for taking her father away, however, it didn't help to remove the numbness in her heart.

She was a 15-year-old teenager who lived for the weekends when she could go out to parties. She pushed the boundaries more and more and whilst out partying, she would often end up in situations that would open the doors to physical and emotional abuse! The serious relationships she had were unhappy however, she clung on to them trying to somehow find that love and acceptance that she craved for. Although she knew deep down that God was real, she still would not allow him to be real to her. It never occurred to her that the Lord would be remotely interested in her, unless she sat in church every Sunday and was living a pure life that would make him proud of her. She knows now that this is not true!

When she reached her twenties she got involved in a relationship that she treasured more than anything else in life. As far as she was concerned this was real love and this was the man she was going to marry! So when it all eventually fell apart, Emma's despair and rejection grew like never before. There was no hope in her heart for the future. She was at rock bottom and she knew she couldn't carry on living the same way! As tears poured down her face and feeling emptier than ever before, she turned to the God she had heard about since her childhood. In her desperation and deep hurt, she cried out for God to help her and heal her aching heart and he did! She immediately had a deep sense of peace and realised for the first time that even though she had not been remotely interested in God, he had never ever left her. He had been with her through all the pain and all the traumas. She began to understand that God didn't want her to attend church out of some religious duty, but that he wanted her to really know him and experience his love and forgiveness. PSALM 65:3 says, *'When we were overwhelmed by sins, you forgave our transgressions'*. She began to discover that despite the less than perfect life she lived, he had never stopped loving her. She began to understand that God wanted to remove the pain from the abuse that she had received from others and from that day she started on a journey that would lead to her ultimate healing.

Emma is now 27 years of age and has spent the last 4 years training and performing as a dancer in ngm. She says, *"My life has been completely transformed through that encounter with God. He is healing me from past hurts more and more every single day. I know my future is secure in him and I love living God's plan for my life. When things go wrong as they sometimes do, he is the one I turn to for the help I need. Every day, I allow God to direct my life and through submitting to him, I now get to do what I have always loved all along – dance! During my first year in ngm, I was in the cast of the hit musical, 'Luv Esther' and am now a member of ngm's street dance crew, 'Release'. I travel throughout the UK performing in schools, churches and events and even get to share my story at the many places where we perform. Through ngm, I also have met my partner for life and during 2012, I married someone who not only loves me, but also shares my passion and faith in God. Life is still hard at times, but I now live for Him and that means constant security. I know God loves me immensely and that I am his delight but I also know that he deeply and unconditionally loves you too!"*

SPIRITUAL EXERCISES

Memorise Psalm 16:11 (English Standard Version)

In your presence there is fullness of joy; at your right hand are pleasures forevermore.

Meditate on James 1:17

Every good and perfect gift is from above, coming down from the Father of the heavenly lights, who does not change like shifting shadows.

Bible Study

Look up the following verses and write them out in full:

     1. 1 John 1:9
     2. Colossians 1:13-14
     3. Luke 6:37

Write down what the Lord says to you from these verses and then spend some time talking these things through with the Lord.

Write a Psalm

Read PSALM 51 – this is a psalm written by King David after he had committed adultery with Bathsheba and his sin had been found out. After reading David's psalm, write your own psalm to God.

Thankful Thought

Thank you for the many gifts you have given and particularly for the gift of sex. Help me to enjoy this gift in the way you intended it to be enjoyed.

Speak out

I am guilty free – because of all that Jesus has done for me!

True **delight**
never fades

DELIGHT

DARE TO TRUST IN HIS DELIGHT

"**W**hen I was a child I was satanically and sexually abused. I was so unhappy that I tried to kill myself." So began a letter I received from a lady who had attended my Spiritual Health weekends in 2012. As I began to read this lady's letter, I realised this was not a letter of pain, but a letter of hope! The lady has given me permission to share her story, but I have changed her name to Dorothy to protect her.

When Dorothy wrote to me she was in her forties, but she shared some of the most intimate things about her early life. She said that at one point she was so disturbed and unhappy about her life that she lay down in the middle of the road and prayed that a car would run over her. The first car that came down the road beeped his horn and she got up, but when the second car came she was determined that she would not move out of the way. The second car screeched to a halt and the driver raced out of his car. He was in a deep state of shock as he realised that he could have killed this child. He hadn't seen Dorothy and nearly didn't stop. Years later, Dorothy believes that God's foot was on the brake that day!

Things improved slightly for Dorothy, as she got older. She was strong academically and put her hope in going to University and getting a career. During this time however, a friend who had also been abused in the same way as Dorothy, was finding life incredibly difficult. She despised herself and hated the things that life had thrown in her direction and so developed anorexia and made several attempts to take her own life. Dorothy was not a Christian at this time, but some friends who were Christians tried to help Dorothy's friend by introducing her to their pastor. Nothing seemed to work, however, because she could not trust God due to all the abuse and rejection she had experienced. She couldn't accept that God loved her and therefore turned her back on him and took her own life at the age of 21 by setting herself on fire! Dorothy was devastated by her actions!

Dorothy went on to follow her chosen career but she could not shake the abuse from her; it seemed to haunt her and follow her around. Everywhere she went, she seemed to draw people to her who would treat her badly. Her self-esteem was so low that it led to several breakdowns and she was admitted to various psychiatric hospitals. During one of her admissions to hospital, she met a lady who was a fellow patient. This lady was a Christian and whilst she was in hospital she led Dorothy to the Lord. Dorothy has not looked back since.

She said, *"Life has not always been easy, but I know God loves me and is with me. He has taken me on a journey of healing and wholeness. I don't know why my friend died and I lived. I used to carry a huge burden of guilt around with me about this, but now God has taken that burden. He is amazing! He has been totally faithful to me. God has done so many wonderful things for me that I could not possibly list them all, but let me tell you about one thing. This still makes me smile to this day! After various careers in journalism and teaching, God gave me a new job. I now work on the same psychiatric unit where I gave my life to Christ, on the same ward in fact! Every day I can bring hope to hurting people who are in a similar situation to how I was. Isn't God good?"*

I have counselled many people like Dorothy who have been abused by others and I have wept with them as they have told me their very painful stories. Many see themselves as worthless individuals and feel that even God has abandoned them. It is only as we go through several counselling sessions that they begin to discover that rather than God abandoning them, he has been with them at all times even during the worst times of their lives, the times when they have been abused and hurt. The truth is that he cries at the sin that has caused them to suffer such pain and agonies and travels with them on the journey of healing.

Many find it difficult to forgive the person who has abused them, but as the counselling sessions progress they begin to see that it is only as they choose to forgive that their own heart can begin to heal. It is wonderful to see them begin to understand that even though they may not *feel* forgiveness, it is important for them to choose to forgive and to continue to do so. As they continue to speak out their forgiveness towards those who have hurt them, not only will their own hearts heal, but also in time, God will help to bring their feelings in line with their words. The truth is withholding forgiveness does not cause the abuser any harm; instead it allows the hurt to grow within ourselves. It's daring to trust God's love and his delight in us that will enable our damaged hearts and emotions to heal; it's then that we will experience his forgiveness and his joy. Forgiveness takes us on a journey to a new place – a loving, peaceful, beautiful, pleasure filled oasis of delight.

DELIGHT
SPIRITUAL EXERCISES

Meditate on LUKE 4:18

The Spirit of the Lord is on me, because he has anointed me to preach good news to the poor. He has sent me to proclaim freedom for the prisoners and recovery of sight for the blind, to release the oppressed, to proclaim the year of the Lord's favour.

Prayer

Write down ways that Jesus has set you free already and write down things that you are still struggling with. Thank Jesus for all he has done for you and ask him to help you walk in your God given freedom in the areas that you still find a struggle.

Bible Study

Look up the following verses about forgiveness:

1. COLOSSIANS 3:13
2. MATTHEW 6:14-15
3. MATTHEW 18:21-22

Write down what the Lord teaches us from these verses about forgiving others for what they have done.

Remember it's a command to forgive, even when we don't feel forgiveness towards another person. The Lord doesn't want us to wait until we 'feel' forgiveness before extending forgiveness towards them. Nor does he want us to wait until we think the other person deserves our forgiveness – this may never happen. However, the Lord wants us to speak out our forgiveness despite our feelings. As we do and keep on forgiving those who have abused or hurt us, the Lord will bring our feelings into order. Not only that, but the Lord will bring much healing into our own lives. If you need to forgive someone, then can I encourage you to do it today? Do not waste another second, but step into your God given freedom.

Thankful Thought

Thank you for the freedom you have already given me! Help me to step into more of this freedom today!

Speak out

I am accepted; I am forgiven. I am a new and wonderful creation

Delighting in the **Lord** releases the **desires** of your heart

DELIGHT

The gift of intimacy

Another precious gift the Lord gave Adam and Eve was deep intimacy with him! We only need to look at the way the Lord created Adam to see that depth of intimacy. It says in GENESIS 2:7, *'The Lord God formed man from the dust of the ground and breathed into his nostrils the breath of life and the man became a living being'*. What a wonderful picture of intimacy at its deepest level. God breathes his life into his creation and because of his breath we become a living being, able to communicate and have profound intimacy with our creator. The truth is that if God removed his breath of life from us, we would die! In ACTS 17:28 it says, *'In him we live and move and have our being'*, which, in other words, means that without the Lord and the life he gives, we would cease to exist. However, because he lives, this means we can live also and experience the intimacy that God intended for his creation in the beginning. The Lord walked in the garden with Adam and Eve and the Lord walks with you! In DEUTERONOMY 31:8 he says, *'The Lord himself goes before you and will be with you; he will never leave you nor forsake you. Do not be afraid; do not be discouraged'*. He won't ever desert you!

Someone once said that when you go above the speed limit that the angels would jump off your car! This statement gives the impression that God is shocked at us when we sin and therefore will leave us to flounder by ourselves. The truth is, that's the time when the angels will jump on the car! You see, God doesn't leave you by yourself when you sin he still lovingly takes care of his creation and holds us in his love. We may not know this or realise this, but this is the truth. The Lord loves each of us so deeply and wants that deep intimate relationship with us. He knows everything about us. He knows our deepest thoughts and desires and therefore is never shocked when we sin. He wants us to begin to know him more so that our desire to do wrong disappears in our longing to be much more like him. We may wander far from him, but he never wanders far from us! His presence is with us every second of every day!

When Ray's mum, because of medical reasons, had to be taken into a care home this was the first time she and Ray's dad had been apart. Neither of them wanted this to happen and fought against it for some time, but gradually Ray's dad recognised that his wife needed medical attention 24 hours a day and therefore this was the only option. They had been married many years and still loved each other deeply. Each day for three years Ray's dad would go to the home where his wife was and sit in her very small bedroom with her. Even though she could hardly communicate with him because of the medical condition she had, he would sit beside her and hold her hand. He spoke to her, he helped her eat; he looked after her every need for many hours every day. He did this because she was his delight! He never wanted to leave her and only did once because he attended a funeral of a very dear friend. He cried many times at home because they could not be together at all times. He loved her in such a deep way. When she died after 66 years of married life he was heartbroken for his friend, his darling, his beloved, his delight had gone! Love means not walking away during the hard times of life and Ray's dad did not once walk away. He found enormous pleasure in just being with her. While she was alive he gave of himself to her in such a remarkable sacrificial way, demonstrating to all around just how much he adored her. He didn't do that because he had to, he did it because he wanted to; he loved her so much.

His love is such a wonderful reflection in a small way of how much God loves every single one of us. He won't leave us when times are bad, he is always there showing us how much he cares. Even the smallest cry for help he will hear because he is so close to each of us. Like Ray's dad he doesn't leave because the place you are in is not to his liking. You see, God is not frightened of sin! It doesn't matter where you are, because he loves and adores you and wants to remain with you. He doesn't stay because he has to; he stays because he wants to!

Oasis of DELIGHT
SPIRITUAL EXERCISES

Memorise HEBREWS 13:5B

"Never will I leave you; never will I forsake you!"

Meditate on a product of nature e.g., a twig, a flower, an apple or a fruit of some kind, water etc. Ask God what he wants to say to you through this object.

Paraphrase SONG OF SONGS 2:10-13

My lover spoke and said to me, "Arise, my darling, my beautiful one and come with me. See! The winter is past; the rains are over and gone. Flowers appear on the earth; the season of singing has come, the cooing of doves is heard in our land. The fig tree forms its early fruit; the blossoming vines spread their fragrance. Arise, come, my darling; my beautiful one, come with me"

Write a Psalm

Write a psalm to God about your desire for deep intimacy with him.

Thankful Thought

Thank you that the God of the universe loves my company. Thank you that you love hanging out with me!

Speak Out ISAIAH 61:10A

I delight greatly in the Lord; my soul rejoices in my God.

Delight remains when you **know** you are **loved**

DELIGHT

HE KNOWS MY NAME!

Just recently Ray and I had the privilege of going to a leader's prayer event in the Palace of Westminster. Around sixty leaders met together to listen to what the Lord had to say about our nation. Whilst there, we met some leaders we had not had contact with for many years. One of those leaders was David Pawson. During the '80's we had come to know and love David and much of his teaching had been so helpful in our early years as leaders. We were so thrilled that we had another chance to spend a few minutes with him. He told us that at the age of 82, he is still travelling around the world teaching people about the Kingdom of God. He went on to tell us that recently he had been invited to speak at a very large Catholic convention in Ireland where God moved in a powerful way. He had never spoken at this convention before and so during his time there he asked the leadership how they knew about him. Their answer took him by surprise. They said, *"An angel told us your name!"* They went on to explain that they had never heard of him and when an angel told them to invite him, they had to look on the Internet to see if a David

Pawson who was a Christian teacher even existed! They found his web site and wrote to invite him to Ireland.

Apart from the fact that having an angel as your promoter seems the best thing ever, the first thought that occurred to me when David told me that story was that Heaven knows David's name. I thought to myself, *"That's amazing! Even the angels know David Pawson's name. Wow!"* It was only later that I remembered that this same thing happened to Peter in the book of ACTS (ACTS 10:30-33). The truth is that the Lord and the heavenly hosts know each of our names! They know yours and they know mine! ISAIAH 49:1 says that he calls us by name! When the Lord sp eaks our name, it is so intimate and encouraging. He knows us by name; his words are not for someone else, they are for us! Our name is not only written in his book of life, but our names are also written on his heart. How wonderful is that? He knows how many hairs are on our heads. He knows the deepest and most intimate things about us. He knows the things that we have never told anyone else. He knows the good and the bad about each of us and he still loves us. He sends his angels to protect us and to guard us in all our ways! Now that really is a WOW!

SPIRITUAL EXERCISES

Bible Study

Look up the following scriptures and write down why the angels were sent and how they helped each person.

1. GENESIS 16:1-12
2. GENESIS 22:1-14
3. EXODUS 23:20
4. MATTHEW 2:13
5. LUKE 1:5-17
6. LUKE 1:26-38
7. ACTS 12:1-11
8. LUKE 22:39-45

Memorise ISAIAH 49:1B

Before I was born the Lord called me; from my birth he made mention of my name.

Paraphrase PSALM 91:9-12

If you make the Most High your dwelling-even the Lord, who is my refuge-then no harm will befall you, no disaster will come near your tent. For he will command his angels concerning you to guard you in all your ways; they will lift you up in their hands, so that you will not strike your foot against a stone.

Meditate on JOHN 10:3B

He calls his own sheep by name and leads them out.

Thankful Thought

Thank you Lord that you know my name! You speak to me by name! You send your ministering angels to guard and protect us.

Speak Out

The God of the universe knows me; he knows and delights in me!

Words from God
bring joy and delight

DELIGHT

LIVING IN THE OASIS OF PEACE

As I mentioned earlier things like worry, fear, guilt, stress, condemnation, insecurity or rejection can stop us from knowing God's delight in our lives! A lady attended my Spiritual Health Weekends and during that time heard what it says in the Bible about how the Lord treated the prostitute, Rahab. I had spoken on how the Lord loves each of us equally and even though Rahab did not belong to the nation of Israel, even though she was a prostitute, the Lord had plans and purposes for her life. Rahab's future began to change when she helped the spies who had come from the nation of Israel to escape from Jericho. She saved their lives and because of that, when the walls of that great city fell down and her city was destroyed, she and all her family were saved. Her home, which was built into the wall around Jericho, was still standing.

However, God didn't just save her life; he blessed her in the most incredible way. Not only did the nation of Israel invite her to live among them as one of them, but also she met and married a wonderful Jewish man and in time they had a child who eventually became the grandfather of the most famous king of Israel - King David. Not only that, but if you look in MATTHEW 1:5 you will see that Rahab is mentioned in Jesus' ancestors. She is specifically mentioned in the line of Jesus. What an amazing God! He delights in us and blesses us beyond what we can ask or even imagine (EPHESIANS 3:20)! He is a God with a huge heart of love for everyone!

When my second son was born, I remember Daniel, my first son, asking his dad and I if we would love him less now that he had a brother. We told him that when a child is born into the family something happens to your heart. Instead of him having to share our love, our hearts would grow bigger to enable us to love him in the same deep way we had always loved him and yet still have room to love his brother in the same way. That is just a small reflection of how the Lord loves each of us. Don't think that because you have done wrong things in your life that the Lord could never love you. Rahab and so many others in the Bible show us that this is never the case.

As the lady listened to the teaching on Rahab she suddenly realised that it was possible to get rid of the condemnation she had lived under for years! She never could accept that God could love her because of all the horrible things that had gone on in her past. The truth that night set her free! Condemnation never comes from God!

Are you living under fear or condemnation? Is guilt, stress or rejection weighing you down? Then you can be assured that it does not come from the Lord. Jesus did not come to condemn us, but he came to set us free (JOHN 3:17)! Take time to sit down with the Lord and if you have never confessed what you have done wrong, then do so and ask for his forgiveness. He will not only forgive you, but he will free you from those things that have caused a huge burden in your heart. Like this lady and many others, you can feel as free as a bird.

When I recently read PSALM 37:1 *'Do not fret'*, these words really spoke to my heart. There are so many things to worry or fret about, yet the Lord has given us a command not to do so. He didn't just give us a suggestion or some advice; he gave us a command about worry! Yet don't you find it is so easy to worry? Jesus said that worry cannot add any extra time to our lives and to be honest specialists will tell us that worry can actually take years off our lives as it can often lead to ill health. I heard recently that the origin of the word 'worry' is 'to strangle' and that is so true! Worry doesn't prolong your life; it squeezes the life out of you!

During 2012 I experienced a deep exhaustion in the very depth of my being. It took all my energy away and I struggled each day to continue to function in everyday life. I began to think there must be something seriously wrong with me so I went to my doctor and she took massive amounts of blood tests. After checking for various serious diseases and every one coming back clear, my doctor advised me to have some quality time off work. Ray and I prayed and felt it was right to take the month of August off and spend most of it abroad. It was the best decision we ever made. Not only did I recover my health and my energies under a blue sky, but I also had quality time to soak in loads of heavenly sunshine as well.

When I experienced exhaustion, it was easier to worry and fret and that only led me to being more tired. One of the verses in the Bible that has always meant such a lot to me is PHILIPPIANS 4:6 which says, *'don't worry about anything, instead pray about everything; tell God your needs and don't forget to thank God for his answers'* (THE MESSAGE). How can we stop ourselves fretting and worrying? What I discovered was that my peace seemed to disappear when I started to worry! During my sabbatical when I was asking the Lord for peace, a quote from Smith Wigglesworth caught my eye and impacted my life. He said, *"Not long petitions, but faith is peace! Where faith is undisturbed - there is peace!"* It all comes down to trusting in the God who delights in us and wants the very best for each of us. If we believe that and we don't disturb our faith, then we will live in an oasis of peace.

If it is true that the God who made the universe has our lives in his hands, then there is no need to worry. All we need to do is trust! Even if the worst was to happen, our mighty God can turn any bad situation around for our good (ROMANS 8:28)! When we trust and believe in him rather than worry, it enables him to work in our situation. Our unbelief will stop the power of God working in our lives. MARK 9:23 tells us all things are possible to those who believe! When we trust God rather than living in fear, worry and strife, our heart will be at peace! I found this to be true in my life.

A lady wrote to me after attending my Spiritual Health Weekend to tell me that the Lord spoke to her so clearly before she came to the conference. The Lord told her through MATTHEW 6:25 and PHILIPPIANS 4:6 that she should not worry. While at my conference, she received a phone call from her daughter saying that she had been taken into hospital with pains in her chest and was having problems breathing. As her daughter had asthma, she was worried and her immediate reaction was that she should go home to be with her. Four years prior to this, her eldest daughter had died suddenly at the age of 22 because of an asthma attack. As she considered what to do, a still small voice said, *"Do not worry, I am with your daughter"*. She heard those words and believed them and so decided to stay, call several of her church leaders and ask them and her church to stand with her in prayer for her daughter. She held on to the Lord's word and trusted that he would work in the situation.

A couple of hours later she got a text from her daughter saying she had been discharged from hospital and had been diagnosed with acid reflux. Worry could have sent her home despite hearing God's word, but as she clung on to him and trusted that her daughter was safe in his hands, the Lord showed her that he was with her.

It is so easy to worry, but we must realise that the root of worry is unbelief. Let's repent of our worries and fears and choose to trust God. Let's not disturb our faith but choose instead to rest on the shoulders of the one who is faithful and who is worthy of our trust.

SPIRITUAL EXERCISES

Bible Study - Read MATTHEW 6:25-34 and answer the following questions:

> 1. List all the things that Jesus tells us not to worry about.
>
> 2. Now put beside each worry the reason Jesus says we should not worry.
>
> 3. List anything in your life that you spend time worrying about.
>
> 4. Spend a few minutes bringing all these worries to Jesus, repent of your unbelief and thank him for carrying your burdens. Ask him to help you to choose to trust and live with undisturbed faith.

Paraphrase MATTHEW 6:25-34

"Therefore I tell you, do not worry about your life, what you will eat or drink; or about your body, what you will wear. Is not life more important than food, and the body more important than clothes? Look at the birds of the air; they do not sow or reap or store away in barns, and yet your heavenly Father feeds them. Are you not much more valuable than they? Who of you by worrying can add a single hour to his life? And why do you worry about clothes? See how the lilies of the field grow. They do not labour or spin. Yet I tell you that not even Solomon in all his splendour was dressed like one of these. If that is how God clothes the grass of the field, which is here today and tomorrow is thrown into the fire, will he not much more clothe you, O you of little faith? So do not worry, saying, 'What shall we eat?' 'Or what shall we drink?' 'Or what shall we wear?' For the pagans run after all these things, and your heavenly Father knows that you need them. But seek first his kingdom and his righteousness, and all these things will be given to you as well. Therefore do not worry about tomorrow, for tomorrow will worry about itself. Each day has enough trouble of its own."

Meditate on 1 PETER 5:7

Cast all your anxiety on him because he cares for you.

Thankful Thought

Thank you that as I cast my burdens, fears, worries, concerns upon you and choose to trust you, you will carry them and work everything out for my good.

Speak Out

I choose to trust you! My confidence is in you! You are good all the time.

When **delight overflows** in the Lord and my **soul rejoices** in my God, I have **everything I need**

DELIGHT

THE GIFT OF CHOICE!

I couldn't believe I had fainted in a jewellers' shop in Glasgow as Ray and I were picking my engagement ring! I had started a friendship with Ray two years previously when I was only 16, and here I was at the age of 18 ready to get engaged. We only needed the ring! Ray took me to a special jewellery store where I was to pick the ring of my choice. As we spent time looking at various rings for each other, I suddenly felt light-headed and said to Ray, *"Oh no, I am going to faint!"* I'm sure he thought at the time that I was joking, but before I could say anymore, I collapsed! I don't know who was more embarrassed, Ray or I! I regained consciousness with my head between my knees, looking as white as a sheet! My romantic day would always remain in my memory, but not necessarily for the right reason!

Ray and I had met in the back seat of a bus! My father and I had a joint venture happening every year, where he organised a couple of buses to go to a Gospel concert in the Usher Hall in Edinburgh and I sold most of the tickets to my friends! I had heard about this 'Raymond Goudie' (as he was called in those days) who was a drummer from Prestwick but had never actually met him. Someone sold him a ticket and so we met on the back seat of a bus going to the Usher Hall. Never in a million years did I think at that stage that I would marry Ray, after all I was only 14 years of age! However, I do remember almost a year later having a conversation with my best friend who asked me if there was anyone I knew that I could see myself marrying in the future. My answer was that I couldn't see myself marrying anyone I knew, apart from Ray Goudie! I hadn't even dated him at the time!

A few months after this conversation, I met and started a relationship with a boy from Irvine called Campbell. He was my first serious relationship and it lasted a year! We were very close and despite the fact that we were really young throughout our year together, we talked about eventually getting married. He was a really nice guy who was very kind and considerate. He would bring flowers or chocolates for my mum when he came to pick me up and would spend time talking with her while he was waiting for me to be ready. I even remember him coming to our home one day, when both my mum and I were ill and making us a meal. However, even though we shared so much, we liked the same things and we had the same values and Christian beliefs, because I was not yet sixteen, I felt I was too young to have such a serious relationship and so I broke the relationship off. At the time, I wasn't ready to be tied down, but in the back of my mind I truly thought eventually I would marry Campbell. Not only did I really like him but also my mum thought he was wonderful.

One of the brilliant things about my teenage years was that we had a huge crowd of friends who were all Christians. We often met each other at area wide church meetings and youth events. It was at several of these youth events or clubs that I really got to know Ray. Not only was Ray a good looking guy who had a car (a huge plus in those days!) but he also was a bit of a celebrity as he was a drummer in a band. He would often ask me if I wanted a lift home and although our friendship at that time was only platonic, we would spend time talking to each other sometimes for hours. I found it so easy to share even my inner thoughts with Ray. He quickly became my best friend and from there the relationship grew.

The relationship with my mum however did not proceed as quickly as it had with Campbell. Rather than come in and see my parents, bring flowers or chocolates to my mum, Ray would arrive outside my home in his car and just beep the horn! However,

Ray won my heart and my mum's too eventually! Throughout the next two years he would often ask me to marry him in a casual sort of a way. I would joke with him and say, *"Yes"* and then a few seconds later say, *"No I'm only joking"* and we would both fall about laughing. You see, I wouldn't get engaged until I knew from the Lord that he was the only one for me. I had prayed about it but had felt no release from the Lord to go ahead. There were many times when Ray would say, *"Come on, let's get married"* and I would always answer in the same joking way *"Yes let's do it"* before adding, *"No I'm only joking"*. Until one day, I really did say yes and this time I didn't say the usual *"No"*, but Ray wouldn't believe me! It took me quite a number of minutes to get him to understand that I really did mean that I would marry him. Unknown to him, I felt the Lord tell me clearly that Ray was the one for me. It was not just hoping but knowing that the Lord delighted in our commitment together that made all the difference to me.

Throughout our married life, we have had many good times, some really great times, some phenomenal times and some very difficult times but here we are just about to celebrate 40 years of married life! We love each other even more than we did at the beginning. The key for us is our deep friendship and our relationship with the Lord.

I am always more than a little surprised at how many people make decisions in their lives without first of all asking God if he is happy with our choices. The Lord wants the very best for each of us and therefore it is wise to ask him if our every day choices are good. God has given us the remarkable gift of free will, but the best way to use that free will is to ask him to direct our paths (PROVERBS 3:6). The choice I made to marry Ray was a good one, because it had Heaven's seal of approval on it, however as we will see in the next chapter it was in the area of choices that Adam and Eve fell into sin.

SPIRITUAL EXERCISES

Bible Study

Read JOSHUA 9 and answer the following questions:

> **1.** We all make many decisions every day in
> life, how often do you bring the Lord into
> those decisions? Give your reasons for this.
>
> **2.** JOSHUA 9:14 tells us that the children of
> Israel did not enquire of the Lord and
> therefore they were deceived. Write down
> what you can learn from this.
>
> **3.** Can you find another story in the Bible
> where decisions were not brought before
> the Lord? Write down what happened and
> what you have learned from this.

Meditate on JOSHUA 24:15B

*Choose for yourselves this day whom you will serve...
but as for me and my household, we will serve the
Lord.*

Paraphrase PROVERBS 8:10-11

*Choose my instruction instead of silver, knowledge
rather than choice gold, for wisdom is more precious
than rubies, and nothing you desire can compare with
her.*

Memorise PROVERBS 3:5-6

*Trust in the Lord with all your heart and lean
not on your own understanding; in all your ways
acknowledge him and he will direct your paths.*

Thankful Thought

Thank you that you give your wisdom to those
who ask.

Speak Out

Thank you for the gift of choice. Help me to
choose wisely each day!

Know the truth
about how much of a
delight you are

DELIGHT

MAKING GOOD CHOICES

The choices we make in life can really affect the way we live our lives. Make bad choices and we have to live with the consequences of our decisions. Make good choices and we live with the fruit of those decisions. Our every day choices can change the way we live for good or for bad! That doesn't mean that because you choose wisely you are not going to experience tough times. After being married for five years, our marriage went through a really tough time and because of that I had a very difficult decision to make. I didn't know at all how it would turn out, but I decided after agonising for many hours that I would trust God despite the problems that were facing me. I chose to trust God not really knowing what it would mean and it was the best decision I could have made.

It all started when Ray told me one day that he was giving up his faith in God. This was a huge shock, as unknown to me Ray was struggling with his spiritual life and living in defeat in his walk with God. Because of this he felt he could no longer go on living life as a hypocrite and therefore decided the Christian life was not for him.

As you can imagine, I was devastated. I loved Ray with all my heart but I could see if Ray gave up his faith, then we would begin to take separate paths and that could only lead us away from one another. I could see our marriage ending with a divorce and therefore I knew I had a choice to make. I could decide to give up my relationship with God as Ray had done and potentially save our marriage, or I could decide to trust God for Ray. It was a difficult choice. I knew I loved Ray with all my heart and the thought of losing him was so distressing, but the option of giving up my Christian walk was something I could not do. As the tears poured down my face, eventually I knew what my answer had to be! Although I loved Ray with every fibre of my being, I knew that I loved God more! I told God my choice was to continue to follow him and trust him for my husband. I know I have told some of this story in my previous book, 'Oasis of Hope', but I believe that it is important to tell it again here.

Unbeknown to Ray, I was determined to pray for him and not give up until the Lord had answered me! Tears continued to pour down my cheeks as I poured out my soul, but unfortunately it seemed as though Heaven was closed. It felt like my prayers were hitting the ceiling and bouncing back again.

The verse of scripture that kept going round and round in my head was LUKE 22:31-32A, *'Simon, Simon, Satan has asked to sift you as wheat. But I have prayed for you.'* I knew I had to keep on praying!

The whole night and the next day passed without Heaven answering. Around five o'clock in the afternoon, while I was still praying and crying, God finally answered. If he had spoken in an audible voice then I couldn't have heard him more clearly. He said, *"Nancy, don't cry any more. I have seen your tears and heard your prayers and I will answer them. If you could see now what I am going to do in Ray, you just wouldn't believe it. Instead of crying out to me for Ray, praise me for all I'm going to do."* Immediately, I stopped crying. Suddenly my mourning turned into dancing! I danced with joy and delight around our lounge. God had spoken and things were going to be okay.

Ray arrived home from work about five minutes later and in my enthusiasm I told him what God had said. The same cold look that I had seen the day before came over his eyes as he said, *"Well, if God's going to do that, then he's going to have to do it, as I feel exactly the same as I did last night."* From that moment on without Ray knowing, I spent time praising God every day for what he was going to do in him, even though I couldn't see it. I was determined to do what the Lord had told me to do.

It was really difficult at times. There were times when I felt angry with God and I remember hitting the pillow one night as I shouted at God, *"Lord, when are you going to fulfil what you have said?"* Then I would tell God I was sorry and that I trusted him to do it in his own time. Leaving the time and method to God is hard, but as we trust in him we begin to see that he does it better than we ever could do.

It was only much later that I realised that from the moment God had spoken, he had begun working behind the scenes, but I didn't see it or realise it. It was only as I praised God every day that it allowed God to continue to work in the situation. I didn't see even a glimmer of hope until about seven months later and then I could see that things were changing; however, it was exactly a year later when God broke into Ray's life and began to fulfil all he had promised me. My decision to believe God's word and trust him was the right thing to do. If I had chosen to do things in my own way, then not only would the journey have been much harder, but I would have had to live with the consequences of us both being in a dull place with God. As it happened, throughout the following year, the Lord began to call us both to 'full-time' Christian work. I have to say what the Lord originally said to me was so true, because if the Lord had told me then what he was going to do in Ray, I certainly would never have believed him!

Adam and Eve's decision of listening to the enemy and then choosing to eat the forbidden fruit, led them to destroy their intimate relationship with the Lord. There are always consequences to the wrong choices we make in our every day lives.

King David made several bad choices in his life. He chose to lustfully look at a woman while she was having a bath. He chose to invite her to his palace despite the fact that she was married to someone else. He chose to seduce her and make love to her and when she sent word to him that she was pregnant, he chose to try and cover over the wrong things he had done. When that didn't work, he chose to deceive her husband and eventually he chose to murder him. Each wrong choice led to another and eventually God confronted him with his sin. Because David confessed his sin and repented of all he had done wrong, the Lord forgave him. Despite his wrong choices and subsequently having to live with the consequences of his sin, the Lord restored him. What grace! What love! The key to this was David's repentant heart. Repentance means a change of mind which leads to us turning away from the things we have done wrong. The Lord looked at David's heart and knew ultimately David wanted God's choice for his life.

Spiritual Exercises

Bible Study – Read Mark 9:2-8

1. Jesus took his disciples up a high mountain to be alone with him – what does this teach us about our intimate times with the Lord?

2. When an amazing supernatural experience happened – Peter felt he had to say something! What does the text teach us through this?

3. Read verse 7. The cloud of God's presence comes down on those present and God speaks. Obviously the words that God spoke at this time were of major importance. He said, "This is my son, whom I love. Listen to him!" What does this say to you about the importance of listening to Jesus and how do you put this into practice in your every day life?

4. Think through whether you find it easier to listen to the 'lies' of the enemy more than you listen to the truth you find in the word of God and write down what you can learn from this.

5. How does Jesus deal with the lies of the enemy in Mark 8:33 and what can we learn from this?

Meditate on MARK 8:34-35

Then he called the crowd to him along with his disciples and said, "If anyone would come after me, he must deny himself and take up his cross and follow me. For whoever wants to save his life will lose it, but whoever loses his life for me and for the gospel will save it."

Paraphrase PSALM 51:1-2 and 10-12

Have mercy on me, O God, according to your unfailing love; according to your great compassion blot out my transgressions. Wash away all my iniquity and cleanse me from my sin. Create in me a pure heart, O God and renew a steadfast spirit within me. Do not cast me from your presence or take your Holy Spirit from me. Restore to me the joy of your salvation and grant me a willing spirit, to sustain me.

Pray PSALM 86:11

Teach me to walk in your way, O Lord, and I will walk in your truth; give me an undivided heart that I may fear your name.

Thankful Thought from ROMANS 8:28

Thank you Lord that in all things you work for the good of those who love you!

Speak Out a portion of PSALM 43:4

You are my joy and my delight.

God's delight
is unending

DELIGHT

WHERE ARE YOU?

I love the way the Lord counsels Adam and Eve. It says in GENESIS 3 that when the Lord came to walk in the garden with his beloved creation, Adam and Eve hid from him. It was a forlorn thing to do but it's true to say that our natural self tends to want to hide the sin we have committed not only from others but from ourselves and from God. We push the guilt deep inside of ourselves not realising that we are storing up problems for a later stage. Guilty secrets always have a cost! Those things that are hidden will one day pop up to let us know that they are still there. Guilt needs to be dealt with and the only way to do that is to confess it and allow the Lord to forgive you. The great news is that every single thing we have done whether in our past, our present or even in our future has been dealt with at the cross 2000 years ago! Jesus died to set us free from our guilty secrets! Woohoo indeed!

It's interesting to note that even though the Lord knows what has happened with Adam and Eve he doesn't condemn, instead he asks them questions. As Christians we so often condemn! So many people leave the church because we have taken it on board to be their judge and jury. We often forget we are all sinners saved by grace! We forget that the Lord Jesus told us clearly not to judge. In MATTHEW 7 he says, *"Do not judge, or you too will be judged. For in the same way you judge others, you will be judged and with the measure you use, it will be measured to you. Why do you look at the speck of sawdust in your brother's eye and pay no attention to the plank in your own eye?"*

I recently heard a story about how Billy Graham answered a difficult question when he was attending a rally to support Bill Clinton. It was just after Bill's sex scandal had been made public and so the reporter asked Billy how he could support such a man! Billy Graham answered the question wisely. He said, *"It's the Holy Spirit's job to convict, God's job to judge and my job to love."* Oh that we would learn to love others in that way. It's not our job to judge or even to try and convict, it's our job to love people into the Kingdom.

In GENESIS 3 the Lord first of all asks, *"Where are you?"* As I meditated on those words, I realised there was such a deep longing and an enormous ache in those words! *"Where are you Adam? Where are you Eve?"* They were trying to hide what they had done wrong from the Lord, but that is impossible to do!

You can never hide what you have done from God. He knows everything and therefore already knows where you are and what you have done. He is not shocked or surprised at your behaviour because he already knows what is in our hearts but the great thing is he still loves us. The Lord not only loves intimacy with us, he delights in it and he knew that Adam and Eve's choices had led to them breaking that deep, amazing, intimate relationship with him. Therefore as he asks his questions, his heart was aching! Eventually after more questions, Adam and Eve finally spurt out their version of the truth.

It's interesting to note that when we do something wrong, we often look for a scapegoat to take the blame and this is exactly what Adam and Eve did. Adam blamed Eve and Eve blamed the serpent. When things don't go well for us, there is always the temptation to blame someone else.

In the '80's when Ray was producing one of our Heartbeat albums, one of the male singers was finding it difficult in the studio. He was struggling to sing in tune but rather than just say, *"Sorry Ray I am finding this so difficult"*, instead he began to blame Ray. In his frustration he said, *"You are the producer. It's your job to get the best out of me. It's your fault I am singing like this!"* It was true that Ray was the producer, but Ray could not sing the song for him, he had to do that on his own. Ray was already doing everything he could to help him by giving him loads of encouragement and using all the technology of the day, but the singer couldn't cope with his failure to hit the notes correctly and looked for someone else to blame.

With Adam and Eve there was a slither of truth in their answer, but they needed to own their own choices. What Adam was really saying was *"I'm not to blame it's her fault. If it hadn't been for her, I would not be in this position. Blame her and not me!"* It was Eve who encouraged Adam to eat the apple, but ultimately Adam made his own decision. Eve immediately blamed the serpent saying, *"I was deceived; it was the serpent and not me!"* As I said in the last chapter, each of us is responsible for our own choices. We need to be able to own the choices we make in life and freely admit when we get it wrong. No one forced Adam or Eve to eat the apple; they both chose to do so with their own free will, knowing that the Lord had commanded them not to do so.

Let's learn from the way the Lord, out of love, dealt with Adam and Eve; maybe we need to ask questions rather than being the judge and the jury of others. Let's pray for love, grace and wisdom for ourselves and for others.

SPIRITUAL EXERCISES

Paraphrase JAMES 4:11-12

Brothers, do not slander one another. Anyone who speaks against his brother or judges him speaks against the law and judges it. When you judge the law, you are not keeping it, but sitting in judgement on it. There is only one Lawgiver and Judge, the one who is able to save and destroy. But you – who are you to judge your neighbour?

Meditate on 1 JOHN 1:9

If we confess our sins, he is faithful and just and will forgive us our sins and purify us from all unrighteousness.

Memorise PHILIPPIANS 2:14-15

Do everything without complaining or arguing, so that you may become blameless and pure, children of God without fault in a crooked and depraved generation, in which you shine like stars in the universe.

Thankful Thought

Thank you that even though you know the worst about me, you still love me and delight in who I am – Wow!

Speak out

I am forgiven.

Love does not
delight in evil
(1CORINTHIANS 13:6)

DELIGHT

DELIGHTING IN EACH OTHER

I was speaking recently to someone who had been a pastor for many years when he told me about a time when a mum and dad asked him to go and pray for their daughter. She had been self harming and when her parents found out they thought that perhaps she was demon possessed! As the pastor spoke with her he began to realise that this girl was not demon possessed but was hurting deeply inside. She began to tell the pastor things that she hadn't told anyone before and certainly had not shared with her parents. She had been abused in her past and the hurt and pain she had within was the reason she was cutting herself. As the pastor began to counsel her, in time this girl was set free and experienced real healing. She is now married with children.

As I mentioned in the previous chapter we so often judge people without fully understanding what is happening within them. I have been challenged again and again to look for God's prospective in situations rather than just make observations and come up with wrong conclusions. I experienced this for myself a few years ago when someone wrongly judged me. He looked at the circumstances and came up with the wrong conclusions.

Ray and I had been going along to a local church on a Sunday morning when time permitted during the two years that Ray had been going through burnout. (The story of these two years is in my book 'Treasures of Darkness'.) The pastor and the people within the church were really amazing to us. We made some brilliant friends and loved our time there. However, we always knew that our time of attending that church regularly was only for a season. The pastor, who became a very good friend, fully understood this and was very supportive of the work of ngm. When the season came to an end, we knew although we loved the church, it was time for Ray and I to get fully back into the work that God had called us to do. Unfortunately, around the same time the church was going through turmoil from various internal issues and someone mistakenly thought that this was the main reason we left.

Without asking us if this was so, I received a phone call from someone who I had only met briefly. He told me that he had a word from the Lord for me and preceded to give me a very strong negative prophecy, which told me that unless I did what he thought the Lord was telling me to do, then my ministry would be destroyed and God would not bless it. As I listened to his heavy words, my heart began to break. I have always wanted to please God in everything I do, so to hear such a prophecy against me was just devastating. I began to wonder what I had done to provoke such an outburst. Then it dawned on me! I asked the man if his prophecy was based on what had happened in the church and if he thought that Ray and I had left because of it. He immediately said, *"YES."* I explained to him that he had completely mistaken our actions. Although we had our own thoughts about what was happening in the church at that time, our decision was based on what God was calling Ray and I to do. I explained that Ray and I had only come to the church for a season and we had already felt from the Lord that it was time to get back into all that God had originally called us to do before Ray's illness. Rather than ask questions, he delivered a condemning 'prophecy' supposedly from God. We need to be very careful when giving a prophecy that it really is from the Lord and not from our own observations of what we consider to be the truth. We could be completely mistaken. Often those kinds of 'words' can bring hurt and pain to others around us.

Just recently, a church pastor told me that he had been dismissed from his job through a very strong, direct and hurtful letter from his superiors. Rather than talk to him face to face, a letter arrived out of the blue telling him he had to leave! Another minister friend told me he had been sacked from his fast growing church by email. No wonder people around us think God is cruel and unkind! We so need to get to know the Lord and his ways and show others the same joy and unconditional love that the Lord daily shows us. Knowing that the Lord delights in us, surely we need to delight in each other and think the best of those around us.

SPIRITUAL EXERCISES

Meditate on 1 SAMUEL 16:7B

The Lord does not look at the things man looks at. Man looks at the outward appearance, but the Lord looks at the heart.

Paraphrase JOHN 3:16-18

For God so loved the world that he gave his one and only Son, that whoever believes in him shall not perish but have eternal life. For God did not send his Son into the world to condemn the world, but to save the world through him. Whoever believes in him is not condemned, but whoever does not believe stands condemned already because he has not believed in the name of God's one and only Son.

Memorise JOHN 17:23.

May they be brought to complete unity to let the world know that you sent me and have loved them even as you have loved me.

Thankful Thought

Thank you Lord that you sent Jesus not to condemn me, but to show me how much you love me!

Speak Out

God is my delight and I will delight in others.

Delight **keeps you running** when your **natural strength** runs out

DELIGHT

MY OASIS OF DELIGHT

When Adam and Eve were removed from the Garden of Eden it doesn't tell you in the Bible how they felt, but I am sure they must have been totally devastated, as they knew what they had lost. Because of their wrong choices, they could no longer live in their oasis where they had experienced the depths of God's pleasure and delight and what it was like to walk each day with their creator. There must have been deep immense regret and enormous sadness in their hearts. They had lost so much and at that point so did the whole human race. We were created for Eden. We were created for delight. We were created to have a deep and precious relationship with our God and so when Adam sinned, the Lord looked to find a way for us being able to live in the land of pleasure once more.

Throughout the years he sent many prophets to call his people back to himself, but eventually he did the unthinkable, he sent his one and only son to this earth to reverse everything that happened when Adam sinned. On the cross, Jesus made a way for us to come back into that deep and wonderful relationship with the Father. He came not only to restore Eden, but he came to make it better than it had ever been in the beginning. What wonderful news! Yet here we are 2000 years since Jesus died and rose again and so many of us live without really knowing the depth of his love, his delight and his pleasure in us! He has given us an incredible inheritance and yet we are content to live outside of his promises. Even though we have asked Jesus to come into our lives, we choose to live in the land of pain and rejection rather than in the oasis of delight that God has prepared for us. We need to look up and experience his delight, his joy and his love. When we find the greatest treasure ever, we surely will become so intoxicated with joy and delight that nothing else will satisfy!

I read recently in JOSHUA 18:3, where Joshua challenges the people of Israel to take a hold of what God had already given them. He says, *"How long will you wait before you begin to take possession of the land the Lord, the God of your fathers has given you?"* What a challenge to us several thousands of years later. How long will we wait before taking possession of the land the Lord has given us? He has given us an oasis to live in. How long are we going to wait until we possess that oasis and experience real life? He has told us he loves us unconditionally, but how long is it going to be before we know and experience the depth of his love? He tells us in the Bible that he delights in us, yet how many of us live experiencing and relishing that enormous delight? He tells us in the Bible that we are valued and have been chosen, yet so many of us think of ourselves as worthless? The Lord came to bring us freedom; he secured freedom by overcoming sin, death and hell, yet how many of us live in freedom from fears, worries and concerns? How long will we live with our negative words and thoughts? How long will we regard ourselves as useless and worthless, when we have already been given a land to possess, a land where we are loved and adored? Why do we allow our fears to tie us up when we have already been given a land of freedom? How long? How long will we wait?

C.S. Lewis said, *"Indeed if we consider the unblushing promises of reward and the staggering nature of the rewards promised in the Gospels, it would seem that our Lord finds our desires, not too strong, but too weak. We are half-hearted creatures, fooling around with drink, sex and ambition when infinite joy is offered us, like an ignorant child who wants to go on making mud pies in a slum because he cannot imagine what is meant by the offer of a holiday at the sea. We are too easily pleased"*

(THE WEIGHT OF GLORY - C.S.LEWIS).

In 2003, God showed us at ngm something of the depth of his love, which not only changed us, but also made us realise that we had been asleep to the deeper realms of God's glory and presence! The Lord took us to new heights in him and we never want to go back to the way things were beforehand. It was as if we had been playing with the mud in comparison to what we then experienced. The Lord called us to come closer to him and when we responded the first thing he did was to show us how much he loved us. It was as if he woke us up with his kiss of love. We didn't know we were asleep, but we were! We were going for God with everything we had yet we discovered we were missing so much of what God wanted us to experience. As the Lord showed us more of himself, we couldn't get enough of his presence. It was as if he had walked into the ngm premises and into our lives and we had fallen headlong in love with him all over again. We all ended up on our knees crying out for God to take us deeper. We cried for more of him and less of us.

Scenes of revival began to break out at ngm; scenes I had only read about in history books. Each night streams of people came to the open microphone, some to express their hunger for God, some to openly repent of 'hidden secrets' in their hearts and others to tell the Lord how much they loved and delighted in him. We had never before witnessed such hunger for God, open confession and repentance like this. People were lying face down on the floor crying deep tears of sorrow. Their tears were literally causing large puddles of water on the floor as people confessed sins of pride, jealousy, pornography, selfishness, lust, greed and much more. It was an amazing sight, one that we will never forget.

Each of us began to spend more and more time in the secret place with Jesus and as we did our hunger for him and for his presence seemed to know no bounds. We had fallen in love all over again. It was as if we had been born again, again! He lit a fire of joy in us that has never gone out. We could only describe this incredible joy as having a 'woohoo' in our hearts; and we never want to lose that 'woohoo'! We live to see his face; we have to live in his presence, where there is fullness of joy. Nothing else satisfies! The world tries to find that joy in possessions, in relationships, in work, in drugs etc., and although at times we can experience a high through these things, no high can ever compare to the 'woohoo' that the Lord gives us!

Adam and Eve would have experienced the deep and wonderful presence of God as they walked in the garden with their Lord. They would have known what it was like to speak to their God face to face, to live daily in his extravagant delight, unconditional love and enormous pleasure. They would have experienced the sheer bliss of grace so full and so free and the thought of living anywhere else would surely have seemed unthinkable. Once you have experienced the depth of God's love and his oasis of delight why would you ever want to leave? Yet sometimes we allow the sin that so easily entangles us to bring us down to the gutter. Sometimes we listen to and believe the lies and contempt of the enemy. Let's not be happy with making mud pies in a slum when the Lord has an amazing oasis of pleasure and delight for each of us to experience.

I receive many letters every year from people telling me that they have discovered God's amazing love for themselves. They write telling me that as they believed the truth of the word of God and as they sought after him, the Lord set them free. Suddenly, they are able to experience the riches that the Bible says we have been given in Christ. They begin to realise that they are God's beloved people, that they are covered with his grace and that they can live knowing his immense joy and pleasure. They discover that their inheritance is much more than they could ever think or even imagine that it could be! This is not just for a few; it's for all of us! We have all been given a huge inheritance that will take us the whole of eternity to explore, but the Lord wants us to begin to enjoy it now.

In JOSHUA 19:50 it says that when Joshua was given the town of Timnath Serah as his inheritance, he built it up and settled there. There was work he had to do in order to live in his inheritance. The great news for us is that Jesus has done all the work at the cross 2000 years ago! It's been all him and his grace and not our doing! He has placed a huge inheritance into our hands and all we need to do is possess it! How do we do that? By faith! The way to experience our inheritance is to trust that he is a God of infinite pleasure and receive by faith the joy he has for us. Let's walk in his unforced rhythms of grace and discover the incredible, unending pleasure he has for us. We will stop striving and relax when we realise afresh that we don't live in the days before Jesus died on the cross. We live this side of the cross! There is freedom this side of the cross! This fact will not only enable us to trust and embrace his joy and his pleasure, but also will help us to live in the land of bliss, in the land of unconditional love and in God's oasis of delight!

SPIRITUAL EXERCISES

Meditate on PSALM 16:11

You have made known to me the path of life;
you will fill me with joy in your presence, with
eternal pleasures at your right hand.

Memorise PSALM 16:8

I have set the Lord always before me.
Because he is at my right hand, I will not be shaken.

Prayer

Write an honest prayer from your heart expressing your desire to go deeper with the Lord. Perhaps ask him to forgive you for any apathy you might have. Cry out to him to wake you up from your slumber. Ask him to open your eyes and your ears to the deeper things of his Spirit. Once you have written your prayer, then read it out before the Lord.

Thankful Thought

Thank you for the inheritance I have in Christ Jesus! Help me to live in what is already mine every day!

Speak Out

I will not be satisfied with making mud pies in a slum when there is an oasis of delight and pleasure for me!

What an amazing place of bliss the Lord has for each of us. As his joy explodes in your heart and you eat of the fruit of his delight and pleasure, please do write to me and tell me what you have experienced and what great things the Lord has shown you. I would love to hear your story, the good as well as the hard times; the times when you have known his wonderful compelling presence and the times when you have had to trust that he is there for you. I would love to hear your story as you live, eat, drink and dwell in his incredible Oasis of Delight.

SPIRITUAL EXERCISES

THE MEDITATION WORKOUT

One of the lost arts in the Christian world is meditation. However, whenever I mention the word 'meditation' often people get concerned that we are getting into something dodgy! It sounds dodgy because often we associate it with Transcendental Meditation, Eastern Mysticism or the New Age Movement but actually the art of meditation has been stolen from us. Christian meditation is a wonderful, refreshing way of hearing God speak and has been used since the beginning of time.

The Bible has many references to meditation. Let me give you a few scriptures that you can look up for yourself to discover that meditation is completely biblical. JOSHUA 1:8; PSALM 48:9; GENESIS 24:63; PSALM 119:148 all tell us about meditation.

Transcendental Meditation and the New Age Movement tell us to empty our minds. This, I believe, can be very dangerous and therefore I would never encourage anyone to do that. It allows outside influences, which are not always good, to invade our minds and affect our lives. In contrast, Christian meditation is allowing God and scripture to fill our minds. Quite a difference! It demands discipline since our minds find it easy to wander from one subject to another, however, if you are willing to try meditation, I know you will find it a very useful and fulfilling exercise. I have also discovered that for many people it is one of the easiest ways of hearing God speak to you. If you have never heard God speak to you, then do try meditation.

It was back in 1981 when I first heard about meditation. I was at a British Youth for Christ conference when Alex Buchanan, a wonderful man of God, asked us to meditate on a verse from scripture and then informed us that he would pick a couple of volunteers to share what they had received from God. I don't know about you, but when preachers say they will pick a few volunteers, I start to get nervous! In this case, I was even more so, because I hadn't a clue how to meditate. I looked around me to see if there was anyone else as ignorant as me but everyone seemed to be looking intelligently at their Bibles. I thought, *"Great! Everyone here knows how to meditate and I know what's going to happen - he's going to pick me!"* I sank really low in my chair, hoping Alex wouldn't see me and tried to pretend that I knew what to do. There was silence for a few minutes, then Eric Delve, the National Evangelist for BYFC at the time, stood up and said, *"Alex, I'm sure I'm speaking on behalf of lots of people here, but I really don't know what to do. Would you teach us how to meditate?"* As relief flooded through my body, I praised God for his courage and honesty! It turned out that no one knew how to meditate; they only knew how to look as though they did. We were then shown how to meditate and since that time I have used meditation on numerous occasions as well as teaching the practice to many others.

So, how do you meditate? Let me give you step-by-step instructions as to how to meditate on scripture.

HOW TO MEDITATE

1. First of all, relax - it's very easy, so don't get uptight or anxious about it. If you do, then you will find it difficult to hear anything from God.

2. Look up the suggested scripture.

3. Read it slowly.

4. Pray and ask God to speak to you through it.

5. Read it again several times.

6. Spend time thinking about what the verse says.

7. Perhaps dwell on a phrase or section of the verse, or even just one word.

8. Allow yourself to follow a train of thought, until you see something in the verse you perhaps have never seen before or God highlights in a new way.

9. Write down what you get.

10. If your mind begins to wander totally off the subject, then start again.

USING YOUR IMAGINATION IN MEDITATION

Another type of meditation is using scripture, your imagination and perhaps music to bring you deeper into the presence of God. I have often used this form of meditation either by myself or with a large audience. The results coming from this form of meditation have been very exciting. At the end of the meditation, people have often been in tears, having heard from God or having been touched by God in a special way. I would encourage you to use this type of exercise and not to be fearful of using your imagination. It was the Lord who created your imagination; therefore He wants you to use it to His glory, rather than in self-centred and unreal fantasising. Also, when Jesus was here on earth, he used to stimulate people's imaginations by telling stories! If they had ears to hear then they would realise that Jesus was using the story to bring them closer to God.

Over the years I have written many of these kinds of meditations and put them to music. I have had so many people tell me that they have met with God and heard him speak to them through going through a meditation set to music. You can purchase these by visiting *www.ngm.org.uk/shop* or *www.amazon.co.uk*. I'm sure as you use your imagination to bring you face to face with Jesus, you will find that the Lord will use this method of meditation to speak directly into your life and touch you in a new and fresh way.

USING OBJECTS OR NATURE IN MEDITATION

The thing I have discovered over the years is that God can speak through anything! Therefore, I have encouraged people to meditate on nature, a flower, a stone, a fruit or a tree perhaps, as well as ordinary things such as chocolate! When I first asked people to meditate on chocolate I could see people thinking, *"How can God possibly speak through chocolate?"* But, you know – he does! I encourage people to use their God-given senses to hear from God. Perhaps God might speak through the smell of the chocolate, or maybe through how it looks. On the other hand he may speak through touching the chocolate or perhaps it will happen through the taste of the chocolate. I am always amazed at how much people can get through meditating on something like a simple piece of chocolate!

At my weekend conferences, which I hold every year in a luxury hotel in Bristol and Preston, I often encourage people to meditate on the simple things of life. At one point, I asked the delegates to open their handbags or look in their pockets and bring out something ordinary from their bag and ask God to speak to them through it. The results were amazing! You see, God wants to communicate with us and therefore he will use anything to bring his word to our hearts.

Do try meditation but remember that it's important to realise that because the enemy often tries to deceive us, we should always make sure that what we receive from God through meditation is consistent with scripture. Share what you receive with your pastor, spiritual leader or someone who you respect in God, but don't miss out on one of God's unique ways of speaking to us.

WRITING A PSALM WORKOUT

Whenever I mention to the people attending my conferences or one of my spiritual exercise seminars that we are all going to write a psalm, a look of horror appears on a number of faces. Looks of 'You will never get me to do that' and 'well, that's it, I may as well give up now' are common. However, if people take the plunge and decide to go for it, then they discover writing a psalm to be a new and exciting way of putting their thoughts and feelings about God on paper. The first time we did this exercise in Heartbeat, I felt exactly the same. The fact that I was surrounded by people who wrote music did not add to my confidence! However, when I put pen to paper and I concentrated on my 'Heavenly Dad', a great explosion of praise happened within me and I just wrote down what I was feeling. It doesn't need to rhyme or have fancy or flowery words. It just needs to convey your love for God in a way that reflects your personality. As you probably know, David wrote loads of psalms and if you read one you will see that they are more like prayers to God or about God. Be honest in your psalm. God knows all about us anyhow and he really loves us to be honest with him.

THE PARAPHRASING WORKOUT

Here is another exercise that people shy away from and yet when they experience it, they realise how much it can help them get to grips with the Bible. Sometimes we pass over the more difficult parts of the Bible and if someone asks us to explain what we have read, we wouldn't know how to go about it. Paraphrasing can really help you understand the meaning behind the words. Paraphrasing is a fancy word for using your own words to express the meaning of the passage. The Message, for instance, or The Living Bible is a paraphrase of the Bible rather than a translation of the Bible. This is where someone has put the whole Bible into his own words and often this is a very helpful way of discovering what the Bible is really trying to say. Obviously when we paraphrase we need to be careful that we don't change the meaning of the passage but just express it in a different manner. After you have paraphrased a few verses, perhaps look in a commentary to see if you have altered the meaning at all.

THE MEMORISING WORKOUT

When I was a child, I was taught by my parents to memorise scripture. The memorising of the Bible was fairly common then, but over the years this is a practice that seems to have diminished. There are many reasons why it is important to have scripture stored in our minds. Here are a few to encourage you.

> **1.** God has told us to do so. (DEUTERONOMY 11:18)

> **2.** It helps in moments of weakness or temptation; e.g. when the enemy tempts Jesus, he fights back by quoting scripture. (MATTHEW 4:4)

> **3.** It is really helpful when we are sharing our faith with others. HEBREWS 4:12 says that God's word is sharper than a two-edged sword.

> **4.** It is helpful in finding God's direction and guidance for our lives. (PROVERBS 3:1-6)

The main excuse for not memorising scripture is that your memory is bad. However, I love to inform people that your memory can be trained to retain information. It's usually because of lack of use that your memory isn't working as well as it used to.

The best way to memorise is to break the verse into portions. Learn the first portion first, then the first and the second together, then the first, second and third together and so on until you have completed the task.

Let's take 1 THESSALONIANS 5:16-18 as an example. It reads like this:

Be joyful always; pray continually; give thanks in all circumstances, for this is God's will for you in Christ Jesus.

These verses naturally fall into phrases. So, let's take the first phrase: *'Be joyful always.'* Repeat that out loud many times, then add the second phrase: *'Be joyful always; pray continually.'* Again, repeat it a number of times before adding the third phrase: *'Be joyful always; pray continually; give thanks in all circumstances.'* Repeat the same process before adding the fourth phrase: *'Be joyful always; pray continually; give thanks in all circumstances for this is God's will for you in Christ Jesus.'*

Once you have said it all, say it over and over again until it becomes part of you. Why not try recording it again and again and let it play while you are doing other things? It helps to get it firmly implanted in the brain. Perhaps put it on a card or piece of paper and take it with you in order that you can review it during the day. It is worth noting, however, that just because you can say something once or twice doesn't necessarily mean you have memorised it. It needs reviewing in order for it to be imprinted in your memory banks.

In these days when there is so much garbage thrown at us from our society through the media etc., it's so important to fill our minds with God's word. In PHILIPPIANS 4:8 Paul tells us to fill our minds with whatever is true, noble, right, pure, lovely, excellent and praiseworthy, because, as you are probably aware, whatever we fill our minds with eventually begins to affect our lifestyle. That's one of the reasons why it is so important to memorise the Bible.

THE PRAYER WORKOUT

I once heard someone say that prayer is the most talked about subject in the church of God and the least practised! How true! Many people find prayer difficult, yet if we can cultivate a 24 hour a day relationship with the God of creation, then that will be life-changing for us and the world around us. Prayer should never be restricted to certain times of the day, but we should cultivate a prayer life that is dynamic at any time of the day or night. I often have some of my most intimate moments with the Lord in the middle of the night! Prayer is very simply a two-way conversation with God. You talk with him and he talks back. God loves us to talk with him as you would a friend. Tell him how you feel, tell him what you are thinking and bring him into everything that happens in your day. Spend time hanging out with him. Ask for his advice and his wisdom and don't forget to listen for his answers. At times throughout the 'Oasis of Delight - Spiritual Exercises', I have included prayer. I may at times ask you to write your prayer because simply putting pen to paper can be freeing for some people. Jesus had a healthy prayer life; he often prayed early in the morning in what the Bible called 'lonely places'. He prayed with people and he prayed on his own; he prayed as he walked along the road; he prayed in a garden and he prayed whilst he suffered on the cross. Basically he prayed anywhere and everywhere. Let's follow his example, develop a healthy prayer life and see ourselves and the world around us change!

THE BIBLE STUDY WORKOUT

When I was younger, Bible study seemed to me to be only for vicars or ministers with theology degrees and not for someone like me. However, when I started to study the Bible for myself, I was amazed at how much I enjoyed it. As a young girl from Eastbourne discovered, Bible study can be exciting. She wrote to me and said:

"I spent today going through one of your programmes and I have never before got so much from studying God's word. Thank you for giving me a structure which brings the scriptures alive." - J.F.

If you have never studied the Bible before, can I encourage you to try it? The Bible is the most amazing book with many gems just beneath the surface waiting to be found. I know you will find it exciting and encouraging. In this book I have given you certain passages of scripture to study, but have made it easier for you by asking questions. As you answer the questions, I know that God will refresh your mind and bring new hope to your spirit.

It is so important for each of us to feed our minds with the word of God. There are so many things that invade our minds every day and if we don't take time to read and study the word of God then we will never know the truth that can set us free.

You may also be interested to know that I have written Bible reading planners, which take you through the Bible in a year or two years. I started using a Bible planner to systematically read through the Bible many years ago and have found it a fantastic way of reading the whole Bible. When I was young I used to open my Bible and wonder what passage to read. I would discard Leviticus and Ecclesiastes as it felt like hard work and often would finally decide to read my favourite portion of the Bible again! In 1979, I discovered a Bible reading planner and loved it! I have read through the book each year since. Using a Bible planner means that you know each day where to read and before long you discover you have read from cover to cover. I know my relationship and intimacy with the Lord went so much deeper because I was reading the Bible. I would never have been able to start writing books had I not been reading the Bible systematically. You can purchase a one or two year Bible planner by contacting ngm on 01454 414880 or you can purchase it online at *www.ngm.org.uk/shop*.

THANKFUL THOUGHT

For the last number of years, I take time every day to write down something I am thankful to God for giving me. Everyone of us have many things that we can thank the Lord for, whether it is the air that we breathe, the sun that shines, the rain that falls, the house we live in, the bed we sleep in, the food on our table etc. This little exercise helps us to thank God every day for all the good things he gives us. We can often forget to say thanks; so developing this exercise in our lives will make sure that we don't forget. Make sure you read the thankful thought I have written at the end of each chapter and take time to make it your prayer. You could at the same time decide to write a thankful thought of your own each day.

SPEAK OUT

I believe it is so important to speak out truth, especially truth that is in the Bible, which is why I have included this special spiritual exercise. As we speak out the truth, it not only affirms the truth into our own life, but it can also break down barriers in the heavenly realms. Make sure you speak the words rather than just think the exercise. As I have said previously in this book, there is much power in the spoken word. So don't be shy, but speak out the truth and let the truth set you free.

Nancy Goudie's
Spiritual Health Weekends

THREE EXCITING DAYS TO TRANSFORM YOUR WALK WITH GOD

Would you like to be pampered physically and toned up spiritually? Nancy Goudie's Spiritual Health Weekends could be just the thing you are looking for!

Nancy Goudie runs weekend conferences at the end of January and the beginning of February each year at luxury four-star Marriott Hotels in Preston and Bristol. The weekend is for ladies of all ages. Come and enjoy the excellent food and leisure facilities *(spa, steam room, sauna, fitness room and luxury pool)* and also experience God through the inspirational teaching and creative spiritual exercises from Nancy. Special guests include some of the talented ngm artists. Each conference is booked well in advance so please book early to avoid disappointment.

This is a women's conference like no other!

FOR MORE INFORMATION AND BOOKING DETAILS CONTACT:

Zoe Wickham at	Tel: 01454 414880
ngm, Caedmon Complex,	Fax: 01454 414812
Bristol Road, Thornbury,	Email: zoewickham@ngm.org.uk
Bristol, BS35 3JA.	Or visit: www.nancygoudie.com

OTHER BOOKS AND PRODUCTS
By Nancy Goudie

Spiritual Health Workout – £6.99
This unique book is practical, accessible and fun to use and will help you exercise your faith muscles and tone up your heart for God. It is an excellent book for individuals and small groups.

"The depth of Nancy's faith and spirituality are the genuine products of years of walking with the Lord and seeking to serve him – that's why I am recommending her writing to you." - STEVE CHALKE, OASIS UK

HOT Faith - £5.00
If you want to find out about how ngm started or the amazing miracles that happened during their five year walk of faith to get their amazing missions and arts centre (Caedmon) then Nancy's book H.O.T. Faith (Hearing, Obeying, Trusting) is the book for you. It is a book filled with stories of faith exploits and will encourage you to walk by faith every day in life.

"Whatever mountains you need to move, this remarkable book will build your faith and empower your prayers."
PETE GREIG 24/7 PRAYER

Luv Esther - £3.00

This book takes you behind the scenes of the amazing luv esther musical. It's the story of how luv esther came about; how God provided more than half a million pounds and how God visited ngm with his deep intimacy. It is also a study on the life of Esther which can be used individually or in small groups.

"I throughly recommend this book to you."

GRAHAM KENDRICK

Treasures of Darkness - £5.00

This is a very naked and honest autobiographical account of a time when the world around Nancy started to collapse. Her husband Ray, fell into a dark pit where he experienced ill health and burnout. At the same time God was taking their ministry, ngm, through a shift, which caused much pain and insecurity and led to many people eventually leaving. Pressures swept in like a storm leaving devastation, confusion and unanswered prayers. Nancy discovered that through this time there were 'treasures of darkness and riches hidden in a secret place' (ISAIAH 45:3).

The Beloved - £5.00 *(hardback book)*

This is a collection of real stories, poems, wise words, meditations and huge encouragement to know that you are God's beloved child. Any time you are feeling down, unloved, criticised or critical of yourself and life hits you hard, then pick up this book and flick through its pages. Each page is designed to bring you words of encouragement, hope and love.

Confident? - £5.00 *(hardback book)*

This book is for anyone who sometimes swings from being confident to feeling a failure. It's a book full of encouragement, wise words, poems, songs and stories to lift your spirit and get you back on your feet again, ready to face life once more. Through its pages you will feel accepted, really loved and realise afresh how amazing you are!

You are Special - £5.00 *(hardback book)*

In our culture of stress with so much pressure to look good and be famous, we often need to be reminded just how unique, precious, remarkable and extraordinary we are! No matter what colour our skin is, what size we are, what intelligence we display, what background we come from, the truth is each of us is an exceptional human being. In every page of this book you will discover the truth about yourself and realise afresh that you are deeply loved, special and accepted.

Oasis of Hope - £6.99 *(hardback book)*
There are times in our lives when we all need an oasis, a place where we can go and receive a thirst quenching drink for our souls. This book is such a place! A place where hope is renewed and faith can begin to grow. A place that will help refresh the reader physically, mentally, emotionally and spiritually. A place that gives us more of what we need to enable us to keep on going in our journey through life. It is designed to plant seeds of hope into the barren places of our hearts and encourage those seeds to grow and develop so that our faith will soar.

All books are available direct from ngm on *www.ngm.org.uk* or *www.nancygoudie.com* or through *www.amazon.co.uk*

MEDITATION CDs

Peace Like a River - £8.00
If you have ever experienced stress, carried worries, fought fears or are just looking for an oasis in your busy life, then this CD is for you. This recording will take you to a place of tranquillity where peace, love and grace are yours in abundance. Use this CD daily and you will find peace like a river flowing through your soul.

Smile - £8.00
If you are feeling the daily stresses of life, the busyness of work, the pressures of family or just need some soothing for your soul, then this recording is for you.

Both these CD's are suitable for those who are Christians and also those who are not and are available direct from ngm, Caedmon Complex, Bristol Road, Thornbury, Bristol, BS35 3JA, England. Telephone – 01454 414 880, *www.ngm.org.uk/shop* or through *www.amazon.co.uk*.

Nancy Goudie's Spiritual Health magazine
- £2.00 *(yearly)*

Filled with stories, advice, tips and interesting articles – a great glossy magazine to brighten up your day!

Bible Reading Planners – 50p

A superb way of systematically reading through the Bible in one or two years. You can purchase these from ngm or through *www.nancygoudie.com*

Should you wish to contact Nancy
then do write to her at:

ngm,
Caedmon Complex,
Bristol Road,
Thornbury,
Bristol, BS35 3JA,
England.

Phone: 01454 414880
Fax: 01454 414812
Email: nancy@nancygoudie.com
Website: www.nancygoudie.com

Follow Nancy on **twitter** (*@NANCYGOUDIE*)

Join *'Nancy Goudie's Spiritual Health Weekends'*
group on **facebook**.

Like Nancy Goudie page on **facebook**.
(*www.facebook.com/nancygoudie*)